Loco Government!

Chapter I

Class warfare

'Hi guys! So... I'm Rob Cummings and - for my er sins - I'm Head of Communications at Woldwater District Council just across town in Reilly Road. Sandy - oops, I mean Ms Staveley - has asked me to come and fill you in about the work of the Council and how it might appeal as a career option...so feel free to ask me any questions at any time while I rattle on about the main requirements of the, oh... hello, it looks like someone might have a query already?'

Rob could best be described as rather average in every possible way; a bespectacled man in his early thirties with no memorable characteristics to make him stand out from the crowd. He spoke in a mild Middle England accent, had a pale - veering on sickly - complexion and was of medium height (about five feet nine inches in his socks). His fairish hair was already tapering into a widow's peak, and his long drawn face betrayed a rather downbeat mien. To complete the anodyne picture, Rob was wearing a tweed sports jacket with leather elbow pads and a pair of iron-easy slacks which were better suited to a man twice his age. Unbeknown to him, his office nickname was *Fifty Shades of Beige,* and the uninspiring threads that dominated his wardrobe were mostly presents from his elderly Mother, hastily plucked from charity shops or bargain rails in downmarket chain stores.

To his credit, Rob did have one saving grace - in the right light he had wondrously sparkling eyes that were the colour of sapphires .

However, even his prize baby blues were beginning to lose their lustre as the world of work gradually ground him down. The once hopeful graduate who had left university with a BA in English (2.1) in the firm belief that he could make a telling impact in public relations had faded into the ether. Now, approaching early middle age, the glittering career Rob had envisaged had disappeared into the realms of a pipe dream. Instead of impressing big hitters in the world of commerce with grandiose marketing plans and dazzling presentations, he was currently standing in a classroom at the local comprehensive school nervously explaining what he did to scrape a living. His audience - a group of savvy fourteen year olds - were super attentive because they were hell bent on winding him up for half an hour or so.

Rob prepared to deal with the early interruption to his introductory spiel, and focused his attention on a mischievous-looking Colossus in the back row who was waving his hand in the air frantically. Despite a lack of experience in dealing with teenagers, he guessed that the muscular hand waver probably had *form*, and he braced himself for an ominous zinger of a question.

'My old lady goes "dem friggin' councillors up da road is a bunch of crooks, an' dey should all be locked up'. Wha' you say 'bout dat, Blood?'

When the giggling died down, Rob kept his composure and did his best to respond in a measured fashion that (he hoped) sounded like he was *down wid da kids*,

'Well, it's er .. bad news,er bro, that your Mum is not cool about the Council but, if I can just tell you more stuff about what floats our boat at Reilly Road, you might not agree with her putting us down.

2

For starters, I can explain how the democratic process works to stop bad guys messing with people like your Mum...oh, another question?'

This time, a petite and extremely pretty pixie of a girl with long black hair -meticulously plaited - smiled at him and said sweetly,

'Is you like wit' dem dudes wha' my Dad says can't be arsed to fix some dodgy lights in our street?'

Rob was rather taken aback because, for an unfathomable reason, he had anticipated that the angelic mite would have been on his side. Hiding his disappointment, he smiled and tried to respond in a helpful manner, forgetting to try and sound streetwise in the process,

'Well, we aren't responsible for street lighting at District Council level - that's one for the guys at the County Council. But I know that if you report this sort of problem on their website then they'll be pleased to help... oh, another question – yes?'

This time a rather tall sullen-looking boy with spectacular acne all over his face and neck, pitched in,

'Slopin' shoulders, man. Slopin' shoulders. Fix it bro' - just do the job, man. My Grandpops says dat you lot all work from home cos of what Covid done, like, but you're just skiving really and don't do nuthin' all day.'

Rob was used to this sort of populist rant and trotted out what he thought was a smart reply,

'Well, I'm not at home today - er, as you can clearly see for yourselves, eh? And I can assure you all that my workplace is a real hive of activity every day. with really cool people working hard for the community.'

This remark produced a burst of cynical laughter and another hand went up to interrupt Rob's flow. At first, he was inclined to pretend he hadn't seen it, but the chubby girl with the braces on her teeth was jumping up and down, and couldn't really be ignored. Turning to her, he nodded his assent and waited to hear whether she had anything constructive to add to the proceedings.

'There's like this really disgusting mould in our bedroom? An' da Council just gives our Mum lame excuses an' says we need to like keep da windows open? They just goes yadda yadda yadda on the phone, like, an' it's really doin' 'er 'ead in. She's all stressed up, yer know what I mean?''

Rob sensed that this might possibly be a genuine problem instead of another mickey take, and tried to adopt a sympathetic tone when he responded,

'I'm really sorry to hear about that. Maybe you can have a chat with me after this session and we might be able to sort out a way to ......

'Hey Council guy, is you like trying to get off with Amber?'

The bad acne kid was back again, and there were jeers followed by a crescendo of laughter when Amber nipped her nose and pretended to waft away a bad smell at the suggestion of an assignation with Rob.

4

Rob managed to hold his nerve and added as calmly as he could,

'No, no not all. I can er assure you that I only want to help Amber, with her dampness.'

Chaotic noise then ensued and Rob realised too late that he should have just ignored the stupid innuendo about his intentions regarding a minor. He could feel that he was starting to blush and conceded that his verbal pratfall had lost him the battle to win over any of the young hearts or minds in the room - in fact, it was now obvious that he never really stood much of a chance from the outset. All that remained was for him to suck up more juvenile piss taking and then hope that his tormentors would leave the room as soon as possible when the session concluded.
A very long forty minutes later he was mightily relieved to hear the bell signalling the end of his ordeal at the hands of the crazy gang, and he prayed for the arrival of their form teacher Sandy Staveley.

Sandy was a fellow 30-something who he had met a few times socially in local bars and clubs, and was the entire reason for his ill-fated visit to the school. In the wake of a failed marriage in his mid twenties, Rob hadn't had a lot of success with women. He had rushed into a hasty union with Maria, his childhood sweetheart, shortly after returning to his home town from university. Once the dust had settled, the couple soon discovered that they had turned into different people during Rob's absence, and no longer had very much in common. They split up without any real acrimony and still saw each other regularly - perhaps a lot more than they bargained for because Maria was now the Personal Assistant to the Chief Executive at the Council.

Following the divorce, Maria had remarried and was the proud mother of two lovely children, but Rob had drifted from one relationship to another without much joy, and his widowed mother had taken over his life to a certain extent after he moved back into the family home. After a string of fruitless relationships, he harboured an idle fancy that he might stand a chance with Sandy even though she was a smidge out of his league, according to the lads in work. He was determined to plug away at this new romantic challenge, and was confident that he had earned quite a few brownie points by agreeing to have his reputation trashed by a teenage wrecking crew.

To Rob's relief, Sandy came riding to his rescue shortly before another bell rang to herald the start of the next lesson. She was about the same height as him but looked taller because she had a marked spring in her step in comparison with his awkward slouch. On entering the building that morning, Rob had been escorted to his baptism of fire by the school secretary, so this was the first time that he had encountered Sandy in her workplace. He noticed immediately that her long black hair was tied back into a severe bun, which made her face look sterner than usual. He was also disappointed that her shapely legs were virtually hidden by a long Paisley pattern skirt and her bosom was well restrained by a plain white no-nonsense blouse.

This harsh Presbyterian effect was heightened by her distinctive Glaswegian accent which could be heard clearly as she told the class to clear off to their next killing field. The *bad cop* look she cast in the direction of the stragglers made it clear to all the kids that she took no crap from anyone, and the classroom emptied in no time at all.

Despite being taken aback by the change in her appearance and manner, Rob conceded that Sandy was still very attractive if - like him - you lusted over the sexy Nazi prison guard type of women who often appeared in bad war movies.

Eschewing her blitzkrieg-era dystopian expression for a moment, she smiled warmly to put Rob at his ease after his harrowing experience, and was immediately transformed into a paragon of heavenly beauty - or at least Rob thought so. She continued to beam at him as she advanced towards him and gave him a gentle hug of gratitude, accompanied by a small peck on the cheek.

'Thanks ever so much for coming Robster. I know how busy you must be with all the budget cuts and everything, but some of the students were really looking forward to hearing about the chance of work placements and maybe even career prospects at the Council.'

Rob was incredulous,

'I think you've got hold of the wrong end of the stick on that one, Sand. I hardly managed to get a word in edgeways about any of that stuff because all they wanted to do was have a pop at white middle class men in suits – and, even when I did manage to get my oar in, I got the impression that not a single one of them could give a monkey's about working for the Council ... or even working anywhere at all come to think of it.'

Sandy shrugged her muscular shoulders and reassured him,

'Oh well, I shouldn't worry too much, Rob. They're like that with most people who do careers talks .. and there's always the chance that somebody might be interested a wee bit isn't there?   Now, I must make tracks so I'll just let you get on.'

Rob became aware that he was being dismissed by Ms Teacher before he could indulge in a cosy chat about their plans for the evening. When he desperately reminded her that they were going for a bite to eat after work, Sandy just gave him another high wattage smile and said,

'That would be really nice, Rob - but I have a Zumba class at six and then there's a pile of marking to do tonight and – well, you know how it is at the moment?'

He knew a classic brush off when he saw one, but Rob was determined to go down with all guns blazing,

'Sand, you promised that dining out with me tonight would be the deal when you asked me to do this whole careers talk thing last week! You said that if I could chat with the kids for half an hour then – as a *big thank you* – you would come to that Italian place we both raved on about. I've even booked a table and they're really hard to get hold of on Wednesday nights because they do their special *date night* meal deal with a bottle of house wine thrown in!'

Sandy sighed dramatically and tried the amnesia trick while channelling the Nazi bitch look once again,

'Now, don't get me wrong, Rob, but I remember chatting about food and stuff, and yet I can't recall anything about us definitely going out for a meal tonight – and I don't even like Italian cuisine all that much.'

When she saw Rob visibly sag at that point, she relented a little,

'Look, I'm sure I'll manage a night out with you sometime, Rob. Trouble is that my diary is totally rammed at the moment, and that includes taking the Year Nines to the Lake District on a field trip this weekend. Anyway, a young single guy like you must have loads of things to do with your mates in the evening. So I'll call you when I'm free okay? I'll see you later then Robster - and thanks again for talking to the kids.'

Rob knew he was beaten all ends up, so he resorted to a parting shot with a feeble hint of sarcasm,

'Yeah right, Sand. I'll just alert the Beckhams on speed dial that I'm coming over for their evening hog roast after all.'

Rob had set his heart on a memorable evening out and now it looked like he would have to settle for yet another boozy session down at the pub with his young office colleague and his mates. He also had an inkling that his night would probably conclude with a visit to a dodgy curry house, which he would doubtlessly regret in the morning.

Chapter II

Card Bored

The day after Rob got the brush off from Sandy in the classroom, a rather rotund man in his sixties with a shock of silvery grey hair, clad in a pristine pinstripe suit, was sitting in the office of his North Woldchester factory enjoying a very early morning coffee and his favourite brand of caramel biscuit.

Machines hummed gently in the background as sheets of cardboard were transformed into a range of boxes, bags and envelopes for consumers across the globe. Having left school at the age of sixteen without a qualification to his name, Jim Harvey had worked all hours God sent to build his business from scratch. As a result, he now presided over three large manufacturing outlets in Woldshire, having won a string of awards for his achievements along the way.

He had also made his mark in local politics - rising to the position of Leader at Woldwater District Council, as well as being a major player in the Cabinet at Woldshire County Council - and was due to give a live interview on local radio, outlining his vision for economic progress. As he waited for a call from the producer of the breakfast show to activate the live telephone link, he paused to reflect on the highlights of his adult life in case he was asked to provide a pen picture for the listeners.

By the time he had reached his late twenties, he'd followed the path of many budding entrepreneurs in the area, and signed up as a member of the Woldchester branch of the Conservative Party - primarily to make a few extra business connections. He succeeded in broadening his contacts to some degree, but he never felt entirely at home in the Tory ranks and was always a little self conscious about his working class background. This came to a head when he went to the loo one evening at the Conservative Club and, while sitting in a locked cubicle, was mortified when he overheard some young toffs at the urinals mocking his strong West Country accent and his humble origins.

Gathering his thoughts as he came to the end of his ablutions, Jim had made sure that he flushed the toilet with extra vigour while the young oiks were still fooling around at the wash basins, and then he'd shouted loudly from inside the cubicle.

'I could push the button on this flush all night, lads, and I still wouldn't get rid of all the rancid crap that you all spout!'

With a dramatic flourish, he'd unlocked the lavatory door and, without another word to the shame-faced onlookers, he'd walked out of the men's room and continued on his way until he reached his Jag in the car park, determined never to set foot in the Conservative domain again.

He'd still been rather pent up, when he was driving home to his mother's house in Titbury that fateful evening, and he happened to stop at a set of traffic lights immediately opposite the Liberal Democrat Party headquarters. His Mum wasn't expecting him back for supper for a fair while, so he'd turned off the highway and decided to sample what the Lib Dems might have to offer. (In retrospect, one could argue that the Labour Party office wasn't far out of his way either, but it didn't have a cosy little bar or convenient parking spaces. Cynics would also reason that the Socialists usually held little sway in rural counties like Woldshire, whereas the Lib Dems regarded them as very fertile ground.)

To his utter delight, Jim felt very comfortable as soon as he walked into the entrance hall of the Lib Dem nerve centre, having been greeted cordially at the door by a pal of his late father. He'd headed for the bar and had soon begun chatting to a number of younger party members, some of whom knew him quite well because they worked at his main factory in Woldchester.

While they drank their beers, a friendly barmaid joined in their conversation and Jim warmed to her immediately. She was a real looker called Sophie and was just his type - long legs and big eyes - and within minutes of making her acquaintance he had sensed that she might be *the one*. Unbelievably, she seemed to reciprocate.

Their relationship took off from that magical *love at first sight* moment, and when Jim escorted Sophie to a Lib Dem dinner dance at a swanky hotel a few weeks later, a whirlwind romance was well underway. The young lovers were virtually blind to any other person in the room that night, and other guests were already asking them whether wedding bells were on the horizon. Surprisingly, when he introduced Sophie to his mother she was very receptive (which was a miracle in its own right) and commented that they were made for each other.

About six months later, the couple settled into a happy marriage, complete with a brand new mock Tudor house in Upper Titbury. Two years further down the line they celebrated the arrival of the first of two babies in quick succession, both of whom developed into lively and intelligent kids.

Unlike the *let them eat cake* Gentlemen's Club atmosphere that he had encountered within the Tory ranks, Jim's espousal of the Lib Dem way of life paved the way to his hands-on involvement in real life local issues. As part of his immersion in the complexities of those concerns , he began attending several meetings at Woldwater District Council to observe the goings-on. He had noted how representatives from various political parties strutted their stuff to champion their pet causes and - to Jim's great surprise - he became fascinated by the raw cut and thrust of their debates.

These outings to WDC prepared him for his own public speaking debut in the Council Chamber when he briefed the Planning Committee on an application to relocate his Nether Wold-based cardboard processing unit. He planned to establish a new purpose-built factory at Lower Titbury, which was situated on poor quality agricultural land very near to a motorway junction, and he was overjoyed when he gained unanimous consent.

Having won the day, Jim had jumped to the conclusion that his powers of rhetoric had silenced any possible doubters, especially his quips about being *boxed in* at his old premises and the need to *push the envelope* regarding his new venture. (In reality, the approval was always going to be a done deal because the Council owned the parcel of land and it stood to make a very tidy profit from the sale.)

Bathing in the glow of his success in gaining the planning approval, Jim had felt confident enough to stretch his wings further in grass roots politics and, within less than a year, he was selected as one of the Lib Dem candidates when local election time rolled around. He worked tirelessly on the hustings and was duly appointed to serve as a councillor for the Stenchcombe Ward in Woldwater District. Everyone in the party was impressed when he gained a healthy majority and the senior Lib Dems immediately tipped him for bigger things. Jim himself felt like he was walking on air and had never experienced such a buzz from any other venture he had undertaken up to that moment. Even the thrill of being awarded the *Grand Prix du Papier* at an international trade fair in Reims was small potatoes in comparison!

His eagerness to please, coupled with a workaholic zeal and cheery disposition, had compensated for Jim's initial political naivety, and ensured that he gradually rose through the party ranks. Eventually, after stints on several specialist committees (Licensing, Waste, Health and Wellbeing, and Corporate Services) he became Leader of the Council, courtesy of a Coalition that the Lib Dems formed with a couple of Labour Party representatives.

During his climb to the top job at the District Council, Jim had gradually evolved into a pillar of the establishment and he remained well-liked and respected when he became the Leader, despite opening himself up to ridicule at times. His garish suits were always an easy target for the cynics, but he also scored a massive own goal every time his phone rang and Martin Luther King bellowed out his *I had a Dream* speech. Critics would claim that he was a bit of a grasshopper, flitting from one brief to another without really seeing anything through to a firm conclusion, but his buoyant optimism and everyman language were regarded as his trademarks and, ultimately, the secret of his success.

Jim's adoring wife convinced him that he could turn his hand to a wider range of administrative challenges further up the scale. For that reason, he'd grafted tirelessly to gain the Lib Dem nomination as candidate for the County Council's Greater Titbury division, subsequently securing another comfortable majority. Complementing his leadership duties at district authority level, he now held an executive post at County Hall, overseeing economic development.

As Jim became increasingly enamoured with the world of politics, his enthusiasm for cardboard box production had gradually waned, not helped by the fact that his expensively educated son and daughter disappeared into the groves of academia rather than opting to join the family firm. As a result, his nephew did most of the heavy lifting at the factories now that Jim had other fish to fry.

Order books were stable for the time being but there were rumblings about an economic downturn, and his nephew continuously warned him that the situation could change quickly with harsher trading conditions on the horizon. Jim was slowly coming to terms with that grim scenario after many years of healthy growth, and was not at all fooled by vacuous aspirations regarding what he considered to be mythical *Brexit business benefits*.

When Downing Street spokesmen pompously talked up the possibilities of creating *world-beating* trade deals, Jim was staring at the harsh reality of valuable cardboard box contracts in Germany and France disappearing down the pan. Nevertheless, he was a natural optimist and firmly believed that he could help to stimulate growth in the local economy - and in his own business - by drumming up interest in his economic-oriented reforms that were on the launch pad at County Hall.

Jim was eager to spread the word about his initiatives, but he knew that his Head of Communications at Woldwater District, Rob Cummings, feared that his attitude was a tad *gung ho* at times. Rob was too much of an *Eeyore* figure for his liking, but Jim grudgingly valued his opinions and normally had the sense to listen to his advice. In contrast, the Public Relations team at Woldshire County fed Jim's *Tigger* ego on a frequent basis and insisted that he had the makings of a stellar communicator. With this in mind, they had convinced him to appear on the local radio show that morning to publicise his proposals, despite Rob's deep misgivings about the controversial host.

Jim finished his coffee, wiped the biscuit crumbs from his trousers and sprayed his mouth with breath freshener as he waited for his PA to inform him that the radio station was on the line. He had never done a live telephone interview with this particular presenter and, despite his nervousness, he was looking forward to an intelligent and informative debate about economic prospects across Woldshire.

Chapter III

Going potty

At that same moment, Rob was still in bed, hungover after a marathon bout of drinking and a searingly hot curry, all of which had been a poor substitute for his planned romantic dinner with Sandy. He was half awake and considering whether to call in sick when he was shaken out of his slumbers by the strains of jaunty music on the radio alarm which greeted the start of a new day.

'Good morning and welcome to the Kieran Ball show on Radio Woldshire. It's seven thirty on Tuesday 12th September and it's a bit damp out there first thing - but your old pal Kieran is here "on the ball" to brighten things up with cheery chat and a selection of chart hits from today and yesteryear, plus the latest news and weather. Joining us in the studio in a few minutes will be the Leader of Woldwater District Council and also the economic development maestro at Woldshire County Council, Jim Harvey. So if you have any questions for him - or you want to chat about any issues relating to his Liberal Democrat colleagues - I'm sure he'll be pleased to hear from you. Just send your texts to @Woldradio – how about those ruddy potholes eh?'

Despite his wretched state, Rob's brain switched to red alert when he realised that Jim had ignored his advice and had volunteered to be interrogated by the sneaky reptile Kieran. Although still supine, Rob experienced a surge of animation in his tired bones when he suspected that a verbal mauling was about to commence, and he growled at the radio,

'You're a nasty little scheming turd, Kieran! Potholes have nothing to do with Jim!'

Rob could feel the blood pulsing around his body now, and he rose from his erstwhile death bed while the presenter's flowery preamble rambled on. He showered quickly and got dressed (yet another instantly forgettable off the peg suit that his Mum had bought for him in a closing down sale) while Kieran played *Wonderful World*. The presenter then segued into *Dead End Street* which suited Rob's ill humour much better as he swallowed down some aspirin and exited from the family residence without any breakfast. After a speedy dash through the rain, he slid into the seat of his clapped out Ford Focus to begin the commute to work and - fearing the worst - switched on the car radio and tuned into the breakfast time programme again.

' Jim Harvey, County Councillor extraordinaire and also Leader of Woldwater District Council has just joined us. Good morning, Jim – so glad you could phone in to the studio.

'It's my pleasure, Kevin. I'm always erm happy to oblige.'

Rob winced when he heard Jim get the presenter's name wrong and then muttered,

'Happy to oblige, my arse! Jim, why the hell did you drag yourself out of bed so early for the privilege of being hung out to dry by Mr Motor Mouth?'

He grimaced as the cheery presenter blithely ignored Jim's gaffe about his name, and began his demolition job,

'That's the spirit, Jim - as they say in France, "noblesse oblige" eh? But some of our listeners aren't so sure that your Council mates are as obliging as you no doubt are. Over the last few minutes we've had a shedload of texts about the state of the roads, and people want to know what you're going to do about all those potholes.'

'Well Kevin – strictly speaking, issues in respect of erm road maintenance do not come within our purview at the District Council. In terms of potholes, you would really need to liaise with the specialists from the Highways Department at the County Council to investigate the matter in depth - erm, no pun intended,obviously.'

Rob groaned and shouted at the radio,

'And I'm betting that the Highways Department specialists probably told Keiran to take a running jump when he asked *them* to do a live interview. I told you not to do this, Jim - but you wouldn't listen would you?'

Kieran continued,

*'Hmm. I hear what you say, Jim...but you **are** a county councillor as well as being the leader of the District Council, unless I'm mistaken, of course.'*

'Yes erm but my role at the County Council as regards my portfolio doesn't cover erm roads. My specific remit at County Hall is the wellbeing of the macro-economy, underpinned by a suite of new development programmes to optimise emerging skills and promote investment. Now if you would allow me, I just want to explain what...'

'Hang on a minute, Jim, are you actually saying that you don't have a view on a hugely important issue that affects all of our road users? Surely you must have seen the craters that have been opening up on just about every street in our area?'

'Erm, well, Kevin, I know that there is a lot more to do as regards improving our customer offer in respect of erm highways but you must realise that my County Council colleagues in Highways have spent millions of pounds on mending potholes over the last few years and the direction of travel is positive as we continue to....'

'But I beg to differ, Jim - the direction of travel is actually downwards isn't it? Ha ha. You say you've fixed these holes and then they just reappear don't they? Joan of Upper Woldchester says that it's like you're filling them with rice pudding. In fact, when you look at the gunk your contractors use, rice pudding might do a better job wouldn't you agree?'

'Well, that's just erm being facetious, erm Kevin. Look, I realise that the current contractor has not always provided quality solutions in line with the service levels we expect. However, I understand that the Highways department will be re-tendering soon and, apparently, they're confident that they'll secure a much better value-for-money maintenance package. That has to be good news for the hard working taxpayers across the County.'

'Apparently confident eh? Well those weasel words don't fill me with much confidence, Jim, and I expect many of our listeners feel the same way.'

Rob could hardly contain himself and bawled at the radio,

'Oh my Godfathers, Jim – you must be absolutely desperate if you're trotting out your line about hard working taxpayers! As for you, Kieran, you know full well that Jim isn't the best placed official to talk about this road maintenance stuff...'

He was just about to hurl a bucketload of foul-mouthed insults at the host when his car veered violently to the left and ground to a halt, having plummeted into a giant crater that had opened up on the country lane that formed part of Rob's daily rat run.

Chapter IV

Shark Alert

While Jim was being eviscerated live on radio and Rob was struggling to change a car tyre in a downpour, the day was beginning in a more salubrious manner for others. Among them was the newly elected leader of the minority Conservative group at Woldwater, Councillor Ric Sharkey. He was sitting at his breakfast bar enjoying a glass of freshly squeezed orange juice and his home-made muesli while listening to the radio.

Jim's disastrous stumblings and mumblings were music to Ric's ears and he was savouring every moment as he digested his healthy repast at a leisurely pace. Ric's influential partner Nadine had primed Kieran prior to the broadcast and had done a good job judging by his Rottweiler approach. She was away on business in London but Ric was recording the debacle so that she could appreciate the finer points later. When the interview concluded, he allowed a perfunctory smile to light up his rat-like face as he celebrated a monumental Lib Dem cock-up.

His breakfast tasted all the better after Jim's grilling on air, and RIc poured himself another cup of freshly ground coffee to wash it down. Every day he went to great pains to concoct what he considered to be the perfect muesli; he measured - to the exact gram - the amount of porridge base he required, then he added equally specific quantities of fruit and nuts, and topped it all off with a dessert spoon's worth of fat-free Greek yoghurt and a teaspoon of local honey. This daily preparation was a good indicator of the type of person he was - meticulous, methodical, and very boring.

Ric knew that his penchant for precision was not everybody's cup of tea, and he certainly hadn't been very popular with his peers at school because he was so predictably weird. Nevertheless, his forensic approach to life and a facility with numbers had impressed his maths teacher who encouraged him to find a niche in the banking sector.

After graduating from university at the top of his year group, he joined a major high street bank and became a highly regarded financial advisor in a relatively quick time. His metronomic ways and an eye for minor detail were valued assets in that sphere and he enjoyed being recognised as a rising star. By the time he was in his late twenties, he had parted company with the bank and was fronting his own successful financial services company. His old maths teacher had expected him to do well and was not surprised when she saw the progress that Ric had made. But what she hadn't foreseen was that he would also make his mark in the *dog eat dog* world of politics.

Ric's whole way of life changed when he was asked to review the accounts of Nadine Hurley, a freelance advertising executive a few years older than him, who was in urgent need of someone to sort out her haphazard bookkeeping. During a hectic few days when Ric was creating order out of the chaos arising from her mountain of invoices and credit card bills, Nadine began to take more than a passing interest in him. She conceded that he wasn't much of a looker, and also a tad irritating at times, but it dawned on her that he might be exactly the sort of biddable partner that she was looking for - an upwardly mobile *yin* to her power hungry *yang*, as she later confessed to friends who were somewhat bemused by her choice.

She invited him out to thank him for sorting out her administrative mess, put on her best little black dress and turned on the charm in spades over an expensive candlelit dinner. Ric never stood a chance from that moment onwards, especially since this was the first time in his life that he had ever clicked with an attractive woman. Within weeks he was completely in her thrall and contemplating a serious relationship with a new soul mate.

Nadine was very pretty in the right light; doubters would say that her nose was a touch too big for her face and that she exuded a vaguely horsey air, but Ric was captivated by her big smile (perfect teeth - all lined up correctly!) and her sophisticated ways. As their ties deepened, she confessed to him on a boozy evening that she was a dedicated Conservative, just like her parents, and she urged Ric to convert to her cause if he wanted to better himself in life.

What she didn't disclose at that point was that her uncle, Sir Cedric Phillips, was the local Tory MP who had started his career as a councillor at WDC. She had been desperate to follow in his footsteps all the way to Westminster since she knee high to Black Rod. Along the way, however, she fell in with a bad lot at university and racked up a number of drug offences which would have become a major embarrassment had she embarked on a career in politics.

Her aunt consoled Nadine by advising that there was still a path to realising her ambition, through the vicarious manipulation of a proxy. Having engineered the career of her politician husband - a prize booby who was barely capable of doing up a necktie properly - her aunt's advice proved to be extremely prescient when Nadine told her that she was initiating a relationship with Ric. Both women agreed that he seemed to meet most of the criteria necessary to enable the launch of their master plan.

Nadine disguised her subterfuge convincingly in Ric's presence, claiming that her demanding job in the capital prevented her from holding down a district councillor post in Woldwater. However, she suggested that they could launch a spectacular joint bid for political power with Ric acting as the front man while she remained in the background pulling the strings. She emphasised his status as a respected financial specialist, and argued convincingly that he would be an excellent figurehead for their escapade at the local level - and even further up the rungs of power in the fullness of time. Like water dripping on a stone, she gradually wore down his resistance and vowed that she could help him reach the top of the tree in Woldwater, provided he followed her guidance to the letter.

As the relationship deepened, Nadine decided to rent out her cottage in Little Chipping and the emerging power couple moved into a swanky new lakeside home that she persuaded Ric to buy as part of his rise to prominence. She retained her luxury apartment in London and spent the lion's share of her working week there. Nevertheless, she visited Woldshire more frequently, allocating a considerable slice of her spare time to *Project Sharkey.*

Promoting her partner's interests within the local Conservative fold was quite exhausting but Nadine told herself that it would all be worth her while. Because she was seeing Ric more often, she had to endure regular uninspiring sexual couplings with him, but faking orgasms was a small price to pay in relation to the bigger picture that she had in mind.

Eventually, the big moment arrived when she got a tip off from her aunt, informing her that one of the antediluvian Tory councillors was about to stand down from WDC owing to a chronic lung condition. Nadine was assured by her benefactress that a bit of schmoozing on Ric's part would ensure he featured on the ballot paper as the Tory pick when the by-election loomed in the outgoing councillor's Lower Wortley Ward.

Although he was now a card carrying member of the Tory faithful, in truth Ric didn't give a fig about any political party. Regardless, he was always mustard keen to please his delectable girlfriend and he agreed to go along with her zany proposal. He also anticipated that he might generate some additional business via this new string to his bow so he willingly threw his hat into the ring when a list of potential candidates was being drawn up at party HQ.

As Nadine had been led to believe, Ric's nomination was nodded through - thanks to a nudge or two from her aunt - and he began the challenge of campaigning for votes in Lower Wortley. With his usual attention to the utmost detail, he got up to speed quickly on every Conservative and Lib Dem policy under the sun and was not found wanting when he was questioned by voters. Nadine helped considerably on the PR front, and the *dream team* outgunned a strong Lib Dem rival in the by-election, eventually winning by a considerable margin. Ric was surprised when he triumphed so easily, and he allowed himself a cheeky smirk when he recalled that nobody at his old school would have expected the least liked boy in the class to come out on top in a democratic vote!

Nadine was overjoyed when she realised that she could begin her political adventure in earnest. On the campaign trail, she had worked assiduously on Ric's image, recommending a buzz cut hairstyle and a stylish beard to make him look a little older. Once he had secured the seat, she bought him a range of designer threads and rimless spectacles to accentuate a trendy persona. Most importantly, however, she provided Cllr Sharkey with a crash course on the art of public speaking and scripted some of his first speeches to ensure that he made an immediate impact in the Council Chamber at Reilly Road. After many years of marketing soap powder and aspirin to the masses, Nadine felt truly liberated. She was also able to work from her London base more often again now that Ric had been elected, and was aiming to resume her habit of sleeping around without her Woldshire teammate's knowledge!

When the initial euphoria of Ric's victory in Lower Wortley died down, Nadine gradually began to realise that the art of political puppetry wasn't as easy as she had imagined. Although initially nervous, Cllr Sharkey had begun to experience a genuine buzz when he settled into his new role, and was soon charting a way forward to fit his own aspirations.

The Council's Finance Director was the *Top Banana*, as Nadine would say (and, in fact, she inserted that particular phrase into several of Ric's early speeches to make him sound cool) and she made it clear that her chosen man should ingratiate himself quickly with the post holder at WDC. She explained that the FD was the real power behind the Chief Executive's throne because he held the purse strings, and Ric agreed with her sentiment straight away when he began delving into the vagaries of the local authority's finances.

Cllr Sharkey pulled out all the stops to curry favour with WDC's top money man and they soon struck up a good working relationship, having both graduated in economics from the same *Alma Mater*. They spoke the same nerdish language and, during the course of their burgeoning friendship, the FD inadvertently let slip a lot of useful information to his new buddy - something that the poor man later regretted bitterly.

Within weeks of entering Reilly Road, Ric had expanded his knowledge base to a phenomenal extent, and he realised that he was having the time of his life in this strange new environment. He'd twigged early on that Nadine's uncle was the local MP but he saw that as a distinct benefit rather than a curse, and he started to look for ways to exploit the advantages that the link might bestow on him.

Although he played the part of a committed Tory acolyte with the necessary fervour expected of him, on the inside he was nurturing a growing disaffection towards the party's anodyne manifesto, and he was developing his own ground-breaking ideas about the best way to direct affairs. Nadine was so besotted with the idea of moulding him into her ideal Tory councillor that she had no inkling at first about his antipathy towards the party's traditional approach. As his confidence increased, however, he became less of her *Frankenstein* creation and was steadily assuming the mantle of a monster in his own right. She was somewhat alarmed one evening when he suggested that the ideal local government model in the future would be shaped by intense data gathering and managed increasingly through the use of artificial intelligence with very little human involvement.

The first person to spot the emerging danger presented by Sharkey was Rob Cummings, who started receiving increasingly bothersome emails from him. As soon as the Comms Office issued a media release of any import, Ric queried the salient facts with a distinct sense of haughty scepticism. When Cllr Jim Harvey was quoted as saying that the District was a great place to visit, Cllr Sharkey asked Rob's team to provide a detailed list of the attractions which prompted the leader's statement. When the Council advised that free parking would be available in Woldchester after 4 pm to boost trade in the town, Cllr Sharkey demanded a breakdown of the loss of Council income in relation to the increase in trading revenues. A Lib Dem initiative to outsource the running of the Museum of Antiquities at Titbury was almost successfully undermined by Cllr Sharkey after he queried the process for selecting the new provider and then examined all the *hidden* costs. Rob soon realised that any mention of economic issues in particular were like a red rag to a bull, and he began to dread issuing any sort of news release which had a financial slant.

Rob wasn't the only Council officer feeling the pain. Cllr Sharkey (now commonly referred to as *The Shark*) was bombarding every department with queries about their roles and left no stone unturned. He asked the Finance team to provide details of all contractors hired by the Council over a five year period in the knowledge that it would tie them up in mind-numbing research chores for days. At the other end of the spectrum he queried the size of the Animal Welfare team and fired off a range of requests, including whether they had ever issued a licence to rear a tiger cub in line with the legislation covering the keeping of exotic pets!

When the WDC Chief Executive, Vivien Bushby, pointed out to him that these demands were bordering on being vexatious, Ric informed her that he was perfectly entitled to submit exactly the same requests more formally under the Freedom of Information Act and threatened to resort to that method if necessary. Furthermore, he reminded Viv that - under FOI - failure to respond within twenty working days would entitle him to raise a complaint with the Crown-appointed Information Commissioner, who had the power to impose heavy fines on the Council for tardiness.

Elected members of the ruling party at Reilly Road also fell foul of Ric's forensic zeal once he had found his feet, and the relatively affable relationship which had previously existed between the Conservative, Lib Dem and Labour councillors was almost stretched to breaking point by the new kid on the block. Budget debates that used to be plain sailing became a financial minefield as a number of benighted Lib Dem and Labour representatives were ripped apart by Ric's laser-like attacks. They deflected most queries to the

Finance Director in the hope that he would bail them out when they were asked to provide detailed information such as long-term cost benefit analyses and due diligence reports. The poor FD did his best to move the debates along with helpful explanations, but what had once been a rather painless process was now mired in tiresome and extremely time-consuming detail.

RIc, of course, was in seventh heaven, especially when he was chasing up anomalies in the accounts. Any glitch he discovered provided him with a fresh opportunity to ridicule both the councillors and officers involved and make more political capital. At the outset, his fellow Tory councillors were ill at ease with his over aggressive approach but many of them changed their minds when they saw the impact that his challenges were making in local press coverage of WDC affairs (thanks in part to Nadine's good relations with the editorial staff) and the subsequent increase in public support for their party.

A handful of Conservative colleagues were less supportive but Nadine and her aunt were working their magic behind the scenes yet again and had gained assurances from Central Office that the *non-believers* would be de-selected before the next local elections came around.

One of the main dissenters was the Conservative group leader, Cllr Ivan Robson, a grizzled old warhorse from the days of steam power who had served the party since Noah was a lad. Ivan had always been a great believer in positive joint working at the local level and had earned respect from many members on the opposition benches over the years. When several honest brokers appealed to him to rein in Ric, he tried his best but he was in poor health and his appearances in the chamber were becoming few and far between.

Sadly, Ivan suffered a massive heart attack while leading a demonstration against a proposed massage parlour in a leafy suburb of Woldchester, and the need for a successor became a pressing matter when his prognosis turned out to be very grim. There was no obvious choice as opposition leader and - thanks again to more chicanery on the part of Nadine and her family - Ric confidently stepped into the breach, becoming an even bigger thorn in the flesh of Jim Harvey's Lib Dem group, the Labourites, Rob Cummings, and countless other Council officers.

Chapter V

Verbal vicissitudes

Rob was still drying out in his office after a wretched start to the morning following his night out with the boys, and prayed that *The Shark* would not bother him while he was in such a foul mood. Changing a tyre in torrential rain with a hangover was not the ideal preparation for a good day, and Rob's head still ached from his overindulgence in real ale and curry.

He was cradling a cup of hot tea from Maria to restore some life into his numb fingers, and wondered momentarily whether it would be worth his while trying to sue Woldshire County Council for leaving the roads in such a terrible state. He knew from WCC insiders that they had an expensive lawyer who was said to be as impregnable as Fort Knox, and concluded glumly that he wouldn't stand a snowball's chance in hell of getting any recompense.

His negative musings were interrupted by the screech of his desk phone and he picked up to hear Jim Harvey's voice booming out from the receiver,

'Hi Rob - I'm guessing that you caught my interview on Radio Woldshire. Was it as awful as I thought?'

Rob sussed that Jim was aiming for a bit of damage limitation, and opted for a standard diplomatic answer,

'I only caught the initial skirmishes, Jim, then I was sort of distracted when I drove my car into a massive hole in the road that ripped one of my tyres to shreds.'

Jim expressed his sympathy but he was not inclined to dwell on potholes as a conversation topic after enduring the fiendish brickbats and elephant traps that he had encountered during his interview,

'That bastard Kevin told me that we were going to focus on the new skills hub in Titbury. And then he goes and stitches me up.'

Rob took a deep breath and reminded Jim that he had advised against the whole enterprise in the strongest of terms,

'I did warn you about him when you agreed to go on that show. We all call him *Kieran off the Ball* because he likes to play dirty.'

Jim sighed,

'Yes I knew about Kevin's reputation but he assured my advisors at County Hall that he would give me a chance to promote my economic vision – so there's absolutely no excuse for that bugger to take me to task for things I really have very little say over. I'll have a word with the County Council comms team to see what went wrong at their end. They said that he would be eating out of the palm of my hand.... I didn't realise that they meant he would be like a bloody piranha.'

Much to Rob's relief, Jim then changed tack,

'Anyway, that's not what I really wanted to talk to you about. I've got a meeting on the go right now with a chancer called Joe Baxter and he wants to discuss how we manage our marketing and communications - so I think that's more up your street than mine. To be honest, I needed to get away from him for a few minutes of peace and quiet - he's one of those corporate nonsense speakers who love the sound of their own techno gibberish.'

Rob tactfully ignored the fact that Jim had served up a few helpings of cliche-ridden garbage himself during his ill-fated breakfast radio interview, and realised that the leader had been under intense pressure at the time. He now braced himself for a dose of Joe Baxter's chronic patter and could almost taste the *low hanging fruit* dangling from his *overarching strategic framework*. Putting this foreboding - and his persistent hangover - to one side, he asked Jim what the guy was trying to promote.

'He knows all about our efficiency drive and says he can increase our effectiveness by 40% - and he reckons that twelve local authorities have already adopted his scheme.'

Rob had heard it all before,

'Here we go again - a handful of councils have signed up for something, therefore it must be really good. It's usually based on the principle of *eat dog turds - can thirty billion flies be wrong?* and it's nearly always a complete load of bollocks.'

Jim agreed wholeheartedly,

'Exactly, Rob. But Cllr Sharkey met Joe the other week at a tech conference and fell in love with him - and he's urged me to give the guy some face time. Joe's been hammering away at me with his sales pitch for the last half hour so I deserve a breather while he has a go at you instead.'

Ignoring the jungle drums pounding in his aching skull - not helped by the mere mention of *The Shark* - Rob agreed to pop along to the Leader's office and pretend to be interested in Joe Baxter's inane garbage for ten minutes or so.

On entering the room, he took an immediate dislike to the smarmy individual across the table from Jim who rose to greet him like a long lost friend,

'So you must be Rob, the Council's communications whizz, eh? I'm Joe and I'm mega excited to hear about the way that your authority is responding to budgetary pressure situations. I've just been telling your leader Jim here about how we can turbo charge your change mission by transforming your work paradigm using our latest *Dyno Interactive* cutting edge technology. Looking at the bigger picture, our dynamic interface will provide your authority with a full holistic analysis of all your service provision - and this will enable you to identify the most economic MO for delivering a real terms uplift in your BAU.'

Rob's alcohol-soaked brain was beginning to hurt once more, and he managed to interrupt the flow of verbal effluent streaming over his head,

'Hang on a sec, Joe. I get MO – Modus Operandi right? But you'll have to talk me through BAU - that's got me stumped.'

'Ah, sorry - occupational hazard, I'm afraid. So BAU is just Business As Usual - a bit like Situation Normal? Anyway, Rob, what this all boils down to is our USP – er Unique Selling Point – is that we can maximise the labour-saving functionality of your services through leveraging the benefits of what *Dyno Interactive* offers. Here's our latest brochure by the way.'

At this point, Joe handed out plastic bags to Rob and Jim, containing copies of a glossy document, and they took the opportunity to scrutinise the pubication in silence for a couple of minutes as a means of cutting off the salesman's bullshit supply for a while. As Joe looked at their faces expectantly, Rob finally commented,

'Hmm. Interesting... but, unless I'm mistaken, Joe, judging from the photo montage, this looks like you're marketing some sort of snooping device to monitor our staff while they carry out their work?'

Joe looked suitably aggrieved and replied,

'Oh no no. Not at all, Rob! I can assure you that our interactive programs will benefit every cohort in your organisation, basically by enthusing them to increase the range of their work options. From a commercial perspective this is a revolutionary approach to business change....'

Rob held up his hand to stop the claptrap,

'Sorry to interrupt again Joe, but what do the unions say about this uplift of the BAU? We've had a bit of a job getting them onside regarding the modest changes we're making to our organisational structure by introducing joint working arrangements with another council – but your proposition sounds like a totally different game of soldiers.'

'So, obviously there has to be a comprehensive stakeholders' debate around our system's revolutionary advantages – but most work colleagues should know that modern technology moves at breathtaking pace and it's imperative that employers must harness advances to their maximum benefit if they want to stay ahead of the curve. Can I remind you that Councillor Sharkey was in full agreement on this issue when we networked at the National Spatial Data Expo conference a few weeks ago?'

Jim Harvey intervened,

'Well I have no reason to disagree with you about Ric Sharkey's evaluation - and I think I get your drift as well, Joe. Now then, how do you want things to develop from here?'

Joe beamed at them and concluded his hard sell,

'So, the ball's in your court, as it were. But I guess you need to vocalise internally and then we can start planning for your bespoke requirements. In terms of time, we can launch a customised *Dyno*

Interactive system within about twelve weeks once we get the go ahead for onboarding. Of course, Rob, you'll have to draw up a comms plan to reinforce the USP and then we're super good to go.'

At this point in the proceedings, Jim noticed that Rob was looking like death warmed up and he saw an opportunity to wrap up the interview,

'Er, right. Great. We'll let you know then. I can assure you that we'll lose no time in discussing your offer. Thanks very much for coming in Joe, and I hope you have a safe drive home. Watch out for those damned potholes by the way, there's a massive one just outside the exit gate.'

Joe was obviously elated, sensing that he had knocked the socks off his audience,

'Will do, Jim, mate. Now you both have my card and the brochure so I'll look forward to hearing from you soon.'

When he left the room, both men dropped their masks of amiability and Jim sounded off first,

'Dear God! How on earth did other councils fall for this load of tosh? And look at the photo of the company directors in the brochure ...most of them look like the cast of *Love Island*. I suppose we should now *vocalise internally* about transforming our *work paradigm* before we throw this codswallop in the bin. Or judging by the way you're looking at the moment, Rob, you might want to use the bag it came in as a receptacle for your fast approaching vomit show, my old son.'

Rob nodded in agreement,

'Yep. It might come in handy, especially as I have to pull myself together quickly *in terms of time* eh? What a complete plonker! But seriously, Jim, what are you going to tell Cllr Sharkey?'

'I'm meeting the Chief Executive to go through the efficiency plans later this week and I'll ask her to tell Ric that he's done a great job identifying a ground-breaking measure - but we can also make it clear that, as he's the one who has been championing this initiative, he'll be best placed to sell this change to the union. He'll run a bloody mile, of course.'

Chapter VI

Bushbaby blues...

As Joe Baxter was leaving the Council headquarters in his exceedingly large SUV (narrowly avoiding the giant pothole that Jim Harvey had warned him about) a newish Jag was entering the car park. The driver was a haggard looking middle-aged woman called Vivien Bushby, Chief Executive of not only Woldwater District Council, but also the adjoining local authority in West Fordham. This cost-saving measure was the brainchild of the cabinet members of both councils, and they prided themselves on achieving such good value for money. In reality, Viv never knew whether she was coming or going, and always seemed to be in the wrong place at the wrong time.

She observed her weary menopausal reflection in the mirror and decided that she needed an extensive makeover if she could ever manage to grab a minute to herself. At school she had been known as *Bushbaby* on account of her last name , but she never credited that she would develop the alarming dark circles around her eyes that caused her to actually resemble one of the aforesaid creatures. Her hair was greying at an alarming rate and her fondness for all things chocolate was beginning to expand her waistline far beyond the comfort level afforded by her trouser suit.

Viv hadn't been in the best of moods when she began her journey later than planned after trying to umpire a raucous slanging match between her two teenage twin sons. They were both vying for the affections of an attractive girl in their year at school and had almost come to blows over who was going to ask her out. Viv had always hoped that the twins would bond and be bosom pals - a bit like The Proclaimers - but she soon realised that they were closer to being The Disclaimers when they tore into each other on a daily basis. Sadly, there was no longer a husband around to calm things down on the domestic front - Jeff had revealed that he was gay two years ago and was enjoying a fresh start running an antique shop with his new male partner in Netherwold.

She had spent her lengthy commute, listening to Keiran Ball rubbishing Jim Harvey on the car radio, and was now tuned to the follow-up phone-in programme which was equally excruciating from her standpoint. The conversation had moved on from potholes and encompassed a broad gamut of issues related to local government, including late bin collections, delayed benefit payments, and officious traffic wardens aka Civil Enforcement Officers. Vlv felt rather uncomfortable hearing an assortment of bigoted people slagging off her members of staff, but her blood pressure went off the scale when Cllr Ric Sharkey contacted the presenter and advised him that the officers at Woldwater Council were the laziest people he had ever encountered.

Having a pop at the opposition party was all part of the great political game, but council officers couldn't answer back when they were criticised, and there was no doubt in Viv's mind that Ric was well out of order. With grave foreboding, she envisaged her Head of Legal Services, Meera Chopra, having to remind Cllr Sharkey about the appropriate level of conduct expected from a ward member in the public domain. She already knew that it would be a fool's errand because *The Shark* was such an utter twat. In particular, she feared that this latest fiasco would also take up at least an hour of her own precious time because the councillor would no doubt storm into her office yet again and complain about being victimised.

This kind of distraction was not exactly what she wanted as she prepared for her major undertaking of the day - the first in a series of staff briefings on the new *Future Journey* development programme across both Woldwater and South Fordham District Councils. After a great deal of time and trouble, she had convinced the cabinets of both authorities that the savings they were planning for the joint workforce could only be achieved by gaining more buy-in from the officers. The fact that some redundancies would be necessary didn't help matters and was already fuelling their natural anxieties.

Viv had been tasked with sourcing an effective and reasonably priced confidence building programme and had happened upon a package devised by a renowned expert in personal development called Roger Pitt. Despite the smarmy mugshot on his website, she had warmed to the little Irishman as soon as they met for preliminary discussions, probably because he had such an infectious laugh and a marvellous *can-do* attitude. She subsequently attended one of Roger's workshops on a trial basis, and was impressed by his motivational skills.

Once she had briefed him on the future challenges faced by both authorities, Roger could hardly contain his enthusiasm for the task ahead and told Viv that he was passionately interested in working with a public sector client following a long career advising private firms. This confession gave Viv a chance to capitalise on the surprising gap in Roger's CV, and she had successfully persuaded him to trim a good chunk of money off his usual fee on the basis that he could use the results of his labours as base material for a motivational book and video that were both in the pipeline.

Despite her unfortunate start to the morning, Viv was excited about the launch of the workforce development programme, and hoped that the WDC Officers would respond well to Roger's engaging style. As soon as she parked her car and walked into the Reilly Road offices she made a beeline for the Council Chamber as she was running late, and promised herself a large G &T at tea time if things panned out well.

On entering the large room, she was confronted by a rather sullen body of council officers who were waiting impatiently for the session to start. Roger was already at the top table and she hastily joined him, while avoiding eye contact with the employees who were looking daggers at her. She could sense that she was exuding a marked lack of gravitas when she rattled off a brief introductory spiel that she had memorised during her car journey, and then she handed over to Roger dreading the worst.

To her great relief, however, there was a change in the atmosphere for the better as soon as Roger deployed his trademark blarney and then cracked the first of several little jokes.

'Johnny come out of your bedroom now - you'll be late for school!'

'No I don't want to go. Everybody hates me. Give me one good reason why I should go.'

'Well, dear, you are the head teacher when all is said and done.'

A few ripples of laughter set the scene, and most of the audience were soon in the thrall of the effervescent presenter as he plugged the benefits of the *Future Journey* programme. When stripped down to its bare essentials, this merely comprised regular use of an online self-assessment tool to identify and monitor improvements required in personal performance, interspersed with a handful of group exercises to strengthen team building skills. When listening to Roger it sounded like he was handing over a magic key which could unlock the potential to achieve a rich and fulfilling career.

Roger was a showman of the first order, and took pleasure in name dropping some of the high flying clients that he had helped in the past, while regaling his audience with amusing but informative anecdotes that several attendees would no doubt take away and repeat to their families. Towards the end of the session, he invited three officers to come to the front of the room with a view to engaging in a confidence building exercise which involved keeping seven separate plates spinning on sticks. At first, they experienced some difficulty but, once he had assigned them specific responsibilities for individual plates, they were much more organised and drew a small round of applause when they managed to keep the momentum going (assisted by the host who hovered in the background and steadied the odd platter when it was wobbling.)

Roger always believed in concluding with a flourish, and rounded off his presentation with another crowd pleaser,

'You've now seen how a team can work together to deliver results that they didn't think were possible. Well the Chief Executive probably faces even more difficult challenges as she splits her time between two authorities. So I want Ms Bushby to come up front with me to demonstrate how we are going to improve her performance working in harmony with you guys.'

Viv hadn't been expecting this turn of events, but felt it necessary to join Roger as he explained that they were going to carry out a joint exercise. He would represent the staff and join forces with the Chief Exec to keep the seven plates spinning. She was extremely nervous about this prospect, yet she couldn't really back away from the ordeal and gritted her teeth as she prepared for the unexpected task. Roger began the exercise on his own and Viv was gratified that he managed to get five plates spinning without her involvement. She then joined in and realised that she only needed to keep two going which she managed to do quite well after a little practice. The seven plates then revolved smoothly for a minute or so until Roger brought an end to the proceedings.

It soon became obvious that Roger could have kept the seven going himself if absolutely necessary and she was thankful that he was so proficient. It also gave Viv an opportunity to regain some poise for her concluding speech of thanks when she stressed how staff and management all needed to *step up to the plate* to deal with change.

She was pleased with her little witticism and felt quite elated as she left the room to return to her office, conscious of a positive murmur in the corridor.

Viv's day may have started rather bleakly but she was now raring to go, and she gave herself a mental pat on the back as she relaxed in her comfortable chair and drank her mid-morning cup of tea. She had lobbied hard for the cabinets at each authority to fund Roger's *Future Journey* offering, and she now felt assured that her faith in him was going to be justified.

Just as her biorhythms were on an upward curve, Viv's mild dose of euphoria was short-lived - about as long as it took to finish her cuppa - when her PA Maria informed her that the execrable Cllr Charles Horsfield was waiting in the outer office and wished to see the Chief Exec on an extremely urgent matter.

Chapter VII

Armed and Extremely Ludicrous

Cllr Charles Horsfield fancied himself as Woldwater's *King Maker* because his vote in council meetings sometimes gave him a disproportionate influence on local political decision making. The administration comprised 34 councillors, each elected for a four-year term, and there were currently 16 Liberal Democrats, 15 Conservatives, two Labour Party representatives and Charles, who prided himself on being an Independent.

Following the last election, the Labour members had agreed to form an alliance with the Lib Dems and established a coalition administration, governed by a cabinet which was overseen by Jim

Harvey as the leader. Usually, councils with a similar mix of representatives tended to opt for the formation of an all-party administration, but Sharkey had poisoned the political atmosphere so much that Jim and his socialist allies were determined to freeze out the Tories completely, and they offered no concessions to *The Shark* when filling senior posts.

Because the coalition had a wafer thin majority, their policy proposals tended to teeter on a cliff edge when put to the vote. The Leader always had to ensure that there was a three line whip in force to win the day, and maintaining such a slender advantage was a constant source of anxiety for him and his colleagues.

Jim was also conscious that he had to keep his Labour coalition partners sweet at all times and had welcomed Marxist firebrand Cllr Dave Dillon into his inner circle as the cabinet member responsible for Health and Wellbeing. The Leader also managed to swing enough votes in the chamber to establish the other Labour member - veteran workhorse Cllr Keith Wharton - as Chair of the Council, on the strength of his long-standing service and genial personality. The main role of the Chair was to run WDC's quarterly full council meetings, assisted by Nora Allen, the officer who was Head of Democratic Services. Crucially, Keith had the right to exercise a second (casting) vote to break the deadlock when an even number of members voted for and against any proposal.

Having such powerful roles meant that the two socialists had a vested interest in keeping the Lib Dems at the top table, but they also had the means to rein them in when necessary - a frequent source of frustration for Jim and his team.

Charles Horsfield was also a significant fly in Jim's ointment. He had won his council ward election on the strength of creating an organisation that he dubbed the Woldshire Home Independence Party (WHIP). SInce taking his seat, he had become a much valued pawn in the elaborate chess game being played out in the chamber. Ostensibly, the independent WHIP member identified closely with the Conservatives on policy matters. At times this could be a major source of embarrassment for *The Shark's* followers because Charles espoused several ultra far right beliefs that bordered on sheer madness. Ric was especially on the defensive when questioned about WHIP's calls for the sterilisation of all unmarried mothers and compulsory national service for young offenders.

Nevertheless, Ric worked tirelessly to ensure that Charles remained loyal to the Conservative team, and the WHIP member could usually be relied on to bolster the blue corner during crucial votes. *The Shark* was never complacent about Charles's support because his loose cannon associate had made the occasional foray across to the Lib Dem/Labour coalition benches when it suited his needs. Jim Harvey was mindful of the advantages he could gain from Charles's apparent fickle streak, and always went out of his way to keep the nincompoop sweet when feasible. This meant that both Messrs Sharkey and Harvey tended to wear the finest kid gloves when dealing with the WHIP supremo, who was currently standing over Viv Bushby, demanding her attention.

Charles was not Viv's type by any means. She couldn't see any attraction in the weedy beanpole and took exception to his ludicrous pencil moustache and the slick of straggly hair stretched across his balding pate. He reminded her of the *Monty Python Ministry of Silly Walks* character that her father had laughed at when he was a lad, and she always found it hard to keep a straight face when Charles was in her presence.

Although retired, Charles still retained the awkward mannerisms of his previous existence as a martinet head teacher at a local primary school, who had terrorised everyone within his orbit. When the local education authority decided to merge two schools in Woldchester, it was a no-brainer to pension him off early. Hordes of long suffering parents, students and staff were delighted when they heard the news but Charles was furious. His fury turned to a state of apoplexy when it emerged that the new head of the combined school would be a much younger and relatively inexperienced woman of colour. Her appointment accentuated many of the petty prejudices that had made Charles so difficult to deal with, and hardened his resolve to weaponise them via a political route.

In his younger days, he had served as a volunteer with the Territorial Army, and still fancied himself as an expert on military matters. Anyone scraping the surface would discover that, in actual fact, he had been a liability from the outset and didn't seem to understand the meaning of teamwork. He was eventually assigned to menial stints in the TA stores to keep him out of the way, and his commanding officer was relieved when the hapless recruit eventually called it a day.

All Charles's failings in life had been conveniently airbrushed out of his CV in his later years, and a sufficient number of voters in South Titbury had been convinced by his superficial no-nonsense Little Englander bombast to elect him as their ward councillor.

Of late, he had taken a great interest in the Council's annual observance of Armed Forces Day. He was lobbying hard to enhance the ceremony, enlisting the support of both Jim Harvey and Ric Sharkey, who were relieved that he was getting his nose stuck into such a seemingly harmless side issue. The WHIP man was now eager to tell Viv Bushby about his plans and she was somewhat taken aback when he stood to attention rather theatrically, and then saluted her before he spoke,

'Madam Chief Executive - I've been talking to the Coalition chaps and the Tories and we all agree that the Council needs to get more involved in the annual Armed Forces event. At the moment, all we do is invite a few members of the British Legion to watch the office caretaker raise the commemorative flag and then we give the old timers coffee and biscuits, followed by a boot out of the door. Well, it's not really on is it, dear?'

Ignoring the patronising appellation , Viv said through gritted teeth,

'So what do you have in mind exactly, Cllr Horsfield? I haven't got all day so spit it out.'

'Well, I've been talking to the CO at Titbury Barracks and he is more than willing to send some of his squaddies over with an APC - er Armoured Personnel Carrier in civilian terms - to beef things up a bit. We can also invite some of the youngsters from the Combined Cadet Force at the local comprehensive school up the road. Obviously, we'll still round up the veterans but I also want you to issue a directive telling your officers to get off their backsides and attend the flag raising ceremony - rain or shine. Do I make myself clear?'

'Crystal, Cllr Horsfield. I'll see what I can do, but you must realise that we can't just leave the phones unattended at Front of House, and, from a legal standpoint, I'm not sure whether I can actually compel employees to show up...'

'Well, they bloody well should - and you need to convince them! And that's not all, dear - I'm going to lay on a special commemoration of World War One by commissioning the excavation of a trench outside the Council Chamber. I'll get some of the young lads - and members of the fairer sex too - from the CCF to patrol inside it on the day. Attendees will be able to see what conditions were like during major conflicts and how much we are all in the debt of our courageous armed forces.'

'I don't like the sound of kids running around below ground level, Cllr Horsfield. I hope you're aware that we can't risk that sort of escapade unless we get full approval from Health and Safety experts.'

'A mere formality, my good lady. Perhaps your people can organise that eh? It's all coming together as we speak so bear in mind that there's no time for delays.'

Viv was stony faced when Horsfield finished outlining his grand vision but, inside her head, she was wishing that it was already time to go home and she could get acquainted with the large G&T that had her name on it.

Chapter VIII

Planning a panning ...

At the same time as Roger Pitt was building to the climax of his *Future Journey* presentation in the Council Chamber, Cllr Ric Sharkey entered the building and observed the ranks of empty desks in the open plan work areas with a querulous air. He had been used to seeing similar *Marie Celeste* scenes when workstations were deserted during the Covid lockdown periods when most officers were instructed to carry out their tasks from their homes, but nearly everyone had returned to work since then.

Suddenly, Ric heard the sound of laughter coming from the Chamber and, when he peered through the glass door, he could hardly believe his eyes when he saw the Chief Executive and a man who was unfamiliar to him spinning plates and receiving a generous round of applause. Ric was both amused and bemused and, as he sneaked off quietly, he stored away the memory in the hope that he could make some use of the little vignette further downstream once he had done some more probing to find out what had been going on.

Thanks to Jim Harvey's cock ups on Keiran Ball's breakfast show, Ric was in a very jolly state of mind and, during his car journey to the Council offices, he had relished the follow-up phone-in programme on his radio. He was especially gratified that many callers supported the Tory *Hole Truth* campaign - masterminded by Nadine - which called for an end to the Lib Dem's ineptitude when it came to fixing the County's roads. The icing on the cake had been his own personal hands-free call to the radio station, slamming the poor state of the roads. He also trusted that his edgy remarks about the work-shy Council officers had gone down well with the public. All the same, he was conscious that he had roasted a body of people who worked closely with him and would soon get some grief for his act of treachery. Being aware of this imminent danger, he was grateful that many employees were otherwise occupied and he quickened his step to gain the relative safety of the small office near the Chamber, which was set aside for the Leader of the Opposition.

He skipped up the stairs to his haven and began preparations for the scheduled meeting of the Planning Committee. Although he was not a participant himself, Ric was keen to manipulate the input of Cllr Lesley Ashurst, a young Tory acolyte who was one of his party's main representatives on the Committee. Lesley had settled in well and, like her mentor, was proving to be an expert in mischief making. A few weeks earlier when a tedious solar farm planning application was grinding along, she had grasped the opportunity to capture on camera the sleeping figure of Planning Committee veteran Cllr Kelvin Kettleborough. The footage had made its way on to several Instagram and Facebook accounts and had raised a lot of laughs, especially since her caption referred to *the hard working Lib Dem Councillor representing the ward of Sleepy Hollow*. The Chief Executive of the Council had subsequently warned Lesley about her blatant breach of protocol but Ric had praised her to the skies in private and was very satisfied with the progress that she and other Conservative underlings were making to win over the public to their cause.

He and Lesley were amazed that so many of the old Lib Dem and Labour brigade at Reilly Road were so far behind the times technologically. The Planning Committee Chair, Cllr Don Hilley, and other elderly members had no presence on social media at all, and relied almost entirely on Rob Cummings to issue official Council press releases through the Comms Office when they wanted to make any announcements or voice their opinions.

When Ric had mentioned Twitter to the Labour *dinosaur* - Cllr Wharton - in passing, the old socialist had said that he wasn't bothered about bird watching at all and was more concerned about banning fox hunting. Lesley giggled contemptuously when RIc repeated this anecdote to her, and they both agreed that their efforts to make the Lib Dem/Labour Coalition a laughing stock were well justified. On that note, Ric sounded her out on his latest proposal to land another hammer blow,

'There's an interesting planning application coming up for consideration this afternoon, Les. Fifteen affordable homes in Little Chipping on the Wold. Definitely the one to focus on if we want to put the Tory cat among the Coalition pigeons.'

Lesley was utterly confused,

'But this application is a good thing isn't it? I was all set to vote for it, Ric. It's excellent news for ordinary local residents up in Little Chipping, especially as it's so hard to buy decent property in that neck of the woods. And the proposed houses will be eco-friendly so that will reduce water and energy bills for residents. We've been assured that the design will use natural, locally sourced materials and the construction work should create lots of employment opportunities. What's more, the Council is selling the plot of building land to the Nether Wold Vale Housing Association for a knock down price which is why the houses will be so reasonable - so what's there not to like?'

Ric raised an eyebrow and began to enlighten his protegee,

'My partner Nadine found out that a major condition attached to the sale of the land was that one of the proposed houses must contain seven bedrooms, three bathrooms, and a massive kitchen.'

'Why on earth would they need to do that?'

'Because the Council is duty bound to house a very large family currently living in the district. The grande dame of the household is one Karen Craig, a jobless mother who has ten kids, three grandchildren, and a partner called Fred Clark. He appears to be a bit of a drifter from what we can gather; he comes and goes when it suits him, although nobody knows for sure how many of the kids he has fathered and what on earth he does all day.'

RIc paused to let his revelation sink into Lesley's brain and then resumed,

'This extra large family is currently being accommodated in two adjoining semi-detached houses in West Woldchester with a doorway knocked through. It was meant to be a temporary measure but they've been there for over three years and it's not easy for the mother to keep an eye on all of the kids. In fact, the little bleeders are virtually feral and drive their neighbours crackers because they can be a tad antisocial when they're out of sorts.'

Lesley interrupted,

'But - correct me if I'm wrong - even though providing such a big house seems very generous on the surface, I reckon that the

Council should save a shedload of money by moving such a large brood into new accommodation and freeing up two houses for other residents, right?'

Ric conceded her point but emphasised the Council's *Achilles heel*,

'Well, er, yes, it's true that WDC would make some savings.. but the optics are terrible and the Coalition guys have been beavering away to try and keep this bespoke housing solution below the parapet. Nadine got wind of it through one of her contacts and she's passed on her concerns to the Taxpayers Alliance. Naturally enough, they're up in arms and are willing to make a big fuss nationally about the Council subsidising a workshy family and enabling them to live in a luxury home.'

Lesley finally took the bait,

'Wow - a big *sponger family* splash in the national dailies! So let's get this clear - you want me to object on the grounds that this is a bit of an embarrassment even though there is no material reason for opposing it?'

'Too flamin' right. Take the moral high ground and make a lot of noise. And here's the icing on the cake, Les - I've put the word around about these wasters to their potential new neighbours in Little Chipping on the Wold and they're not best pleased. In fact, I've arranged for a minibus to transport some of the current residents to the meeting so they can trot out their concerns about the *Family from Hell* buggering up their lives. I reckon that should go down well with the hacks from the local rags; they normally find it hard to stay awake at the meeting but this will put some lead in their pencils! Some of our foot soldiers are also going to stoke up the rumour mill about people in West Woldchester planning a street party when Karen and Fred's little monsters leave their neighbourhood. It's a bit of an exaggeration but it all helps our cause. '

'Ooh, that's all a bit naughty - but I like it! I never knew anything about this family until now. How did it stay under the radar for so long?'

'My point entirely! And you can really twist the knife, Les, by asking about the lack of transparency on the part of the Coalition. There's no doubt that those muppets have gone the extra mile to conceal their mega house proposal. You'll make Jim Harvey and his mates look like a bunch of softie incompetents - and, naturally, we'll be recognised as the good guys. We have to show that we care about the tax paying residents in the district who earn an honest bob and don't like benefit scroungers. It should be a great day for Tory meritocracy!'

Lesley didn't know what *meritocracy* meant, but she nodded sagely in agreement and prepared for a memorable evening. Not for the first time, however, she wondered how Nadine Hurley had managed to unearth a little gem of information that would catch the Coalition with their trousers down.

A few days earlier, a naked Nadine was relaxing in bed at her Kensington apartment smoking a post-coital cigarette after indulging in a rampant bout of sex with the Labour MP from the less affluent constituency adjoining Woldshire - who actually happened to have his trousers down at the time! They had been irregular sexual partners for a long time, stemming from the fact that she had been introduced to him as a *Socialite* and he had mistakenly heard *Socialist*. She had realised his error during their first encounter but conveniently forgot to correct his misinterpretation whenever they met up for romantic liaisons.

Over the years she had successfully disguised her Tory leanings and had encouraged her Labour lover to brag about his political exploits when they frolicked beneath her Egyptian cotton sheets. He often shared some of the juicy scuttlebut doing the rounds and, as a result, she picked up an impressive amount of useful little tidbits that were sometimes of great benefit to her party of choice. Occasionally, her unwitting informant really delivered big time, and she had been delighted when his pillow talk revealed the damning rider to the Chipping on the Wold affordable housing proposal.

Chapter IX

Shaken ... and stirred

While Ric and Lesley were plotting more mayhem for the Coalition, Rob Cummings was hunched over his desk, steeling himself to tackle a long queue of emails on his PC. He was trying desperately to pull himself together with the help of a couple of Paracetamol but was still feeling horrendously fragile from his night out with the Comms Office junior member Ozzie Burton and several of his pals. The early morning *Dyno Interactive* ordeal with super salesman Joe Baxter had not helped matters and a subsequent unpleasant trip to the gents (where he parted company with the remains of a prawn vindaloo) had made him feel debilitated. He had tried gamely to accompany Ozzie to Roger Pitt's *Future Journey* introductory presentation but had ducked out after a few minutes because he feared that he was going to decorate the Chamber with vomit.

Rob was peeved that his younger colleague was incredibly chipper given that the lad had downed eight pints of lager the previous evening, and he yearned for the days when he used to feel similarly bomb proof. When Ozzie returned from the Pitt presentation in effervescent form, Rob cursed himself for missing out on what appeared to have been a worthwhile break from his normal daily routine. He enquired about the event and Ozzie was full of praise for Roger's presentation style. However, when Rob delved deeper, it became obvious to him that his colleague had been entertained splendidly but had not gleaned any meaningful appreciation of the event's key learning points,

'You should see how many plates that bloke can spin, Rob. And he told this good joke about how many people work at Woldwater District Council - and the answer is about half of them. Do you geddit, eh?'

'I guess so. But what did you think was the relevance of all of this talk?'

'Er, to show that work can be fun I guess, and it's ok to have a good laugh now and again? He told another good joke about a signing event for one of his self help books and a woman in the queue asked him to write the single word *plethora* on the dust cover. He did what he was asked and she said *thanks - that means a lot.*'

Rob sighed heavily and decided that he wasn't up to a long conversation with Ozzie about the art of staff development. Instead, he was in dire need of stimulating his brain to rouse it from its alcohol-induced torpor, and he searched around for something to do the trick. For this reason, he decided to browse through an extremely thick booklet in his in-tray containing all the applications due for consideration at the upcoming Planning Committee meeting, and he resolved to get his head around the vast wodge of documentation.

He was keen to determine what might be of interest to the local press reps who would be attending, and soon figured that the obvious good news story would be the proposal for fifteen affordable homes in one of the most desirable parts of the district. Rob was totally unaware that the Tories were planning to stage-manage yet another publicity coup on the back of such a harmless looking application, and he began to draft an appropriate social media message for the Committee Chair, Cllr Hilley, to accompany what seemed to be the inevitable granting of the application.

While Rob was formulating a suitably bumptious quote for Cllr Hilley's approval, Ozzie was stewing after being put down so haughtily by his superior, and attempted to disrupt Rob's train of thought with a cheeky taunt,

'Hey, Mr Lover Man! I could have sworn you said that you had a date with that sexy Scottish teacher woman last night and wild horses wouldn't drag you out to the pub with me and the lads.'

'Oh, I cancelled the date at the last minute. Sandy was up for it but I could see that she had a load of things on her *to-do* list for school so I told her it wasn't a big deal and we could reschedule.'

'But last night in the pub, when you'd had a good few jars, you told my mate Gibbo that she was a lying toad and had done the dirty on you - and he said that you would tell me all about it today.'

Rob knew that he'd been lured into a trap of his own making and didn't want to prolong the conversation for a moment longer. He tried to ignore Ozzie's query and, in desperation, picked up a copy of an information release that his junior colleague had sent out earlier that morning. Rob scrutinised it extremely thoroughly, hoping that he could pick up a typing mistake or a grammatical error to reassert his authority and thanked the stars when he unearthed a semantic nugget,

'Hang on a minute, Ozzie – am I right in thinking that you've issued this info to the big wide world this morning?'

'Yep, I reckon it will go down well with the public. It's a straight take from our Partner Council's website so you didn't need to check it... Oh hellcats on wheels, there's a problem isn't there?'

'Well it's certainly not what I would have written. Listen to this opening line: *Woldwater District Council is cracking down on dog owners who do not pick up their poo*. Does that sound ok to you?'

'Makes sense doesn't it? Keeps the pavements nice and tidy. And it stops all the kids standing in horrible smelly mess.'

'I guess it does. But it also suggests that the dog owners themselves might be taking a dump. Can you issue a correction and say we are *cracking down on dog owners who do not pick up **poo left by their pets**?*

'Hah, right, I get it, Rob Don't worry, I'll sort it straight away. Well quicker than it'll take you to get things back on track with your cheat of a girlfriend eh?'.

Rob had limited reserves of sparkling wit and repartee at his disposal to counter yet another puerile salvo aimed at his love life (or lack of it) and he was extremely relieved when the phone on his desk chirped into life. He lunged for the receiver like a junkie in need of an urgent fix, and was greeted by the voice of Meera Chopra, the Chief Legal Officer. Apparently, she wanted to see him when he was free to sort out a potential query from the local paper about a controversial parking offence. Taking this as his excuse to leave the room with a shred of dignity, Rob departed hastily, thanking the inventor of the phone for sparing his blushes.

On his way to Meera's office, he could feel a fresh wave of nausea welling up inside him and decided on a detour into the fresh air to clear his head and settle his stomach once and for all. He reasoned that a quick stroll around the grounds would probably do the trick - and might also help him overcome the urge to defenestrate his junior colleague before the end of the working day.

Rob exited the building through the main reception area and enjoyed the warm embrace of the sunshine as he strolled along listening to the soothing trill of birdsong in the nearby trees. Slowly but surely, he could feel his brain cells coming back into whack. He walked beyond the car park and descended a grassy knoll that led to a sheltered housing development which boasted a row of neat little gardens, nearly all of which contained a host of flowers in full bloom. With his spirits somewhat restored, he then undertook a brisk walk along the adjoining canal in the hope that he might see some wildlife. He was in luck when a large heron appeared and he was thrilled to see it dive into the water and emerge with a small fish in its beak.

As he continued on his way, Rob was highly amused to see a long boat called *No Regrets,* which displayed a sign in a window announcing *For Sale - Apply Within*. It was those sort of little foibles that endeared him to the Woldshire area, and he now felt in a sufficiently good mood to begin scheduling the rest of the day in his head as he retraced his steps towards the Council buildings.

Rob was deep in thought by the time he approached the car park again and, as he turned the corner towards the Chamber, he was composing a suitable form of words for a speech he was writing for the Leader of the Council. That was probably why he didn't notice the freshly dug trench until he had almost reached the edge and was halted in his tracks by a blood curdling scream,

'Look out, you bloody fool! Can't you read the sign telling pedestrians to keep away from the verge? Only a stupid idiot would ignore that!'

Rob was shaken out of his reverie in the nick of time, and was confronted by the flushed face of Cllr Horsfield, who was bawling at him at the top of his voice. The councillor in question always took pleasure in berating WDC officers when the chance arose, and he was savouring the opportunity to bully a prime target mercilessly. To further justify his savage rage, Cllr Horsfield pointed to a small handwritten notice pinned on the nearby railings, which read: *DANGER! Please keep to the walkway - earthworks under construction. Authorised by Cllr Charles Horsfield.*

Rob was completely baffled for a moment and was trying to rationalise what was happening. Despite his hangover from Hades, he was certain that there hadn't been a mini digger, piles of earth and three workmen clad in orange overalls when he had driven into

60

the Reilly Road car park a few hours earlier. He therefore figured that the excavation hadn't been underway too long, and he also assumed that Cllr Horsfield was overseeing the task himself because the pillock was hovering at the side of a hole in the ground. He was sporting a small hard hat which made him look like he had the glans of a penis on his head, and had donned some serge blue dungarees and a high-viz jacket over his business suit. Needless to say, he was wearing a pair of wellington boots to protect himself from the muck flying around his ankles while the project took shape.

Rob was no style guru himself, but it occurred to him that, whatever outfit Charles Horsfield wore, he would always manage to look like a Grade One arsehole. Strictly speaking, Council officers were not permitted to answer back when elected officials criticised them, but Rob couldn't resist having a pop at his persecutor after narrowly avoiding a nasty tumble into the abyss,

'I beg your pardon for not seeing a sign that is the size of an amoeba's manhood, Cllr Horsfield. It isn't exactly obvious is it? And what's going on here, anyway? Are we under siege or something? An excavation of this size is normally crawling with regulatory bods checking that everything is okay, so why aren't they here? This looks like a bit of a disaster waiting to happen, don't you think?'

Cllr Horsfield bristled at the insolent tone of a man he regarded as an insubstantial council lackey, and vowed to lodge a formal complaint to the Chief Exec about Rob's insubordinate attitude,

'I don't like your style, laddie. If wimps like you had started moaning about regulations back in the day we would never have won either of the two World Wars! There's more to life than red tape you know.'

The councillor was gearing up to launch a further tirade, when it suddenly occurred to him that getting the comms guy onside might be a good idea, even though he didn't like the cut of his jib. Taking what he considered to be a more conciliatory tone, he provided a bit of background for Rob's benefit,

'Look, er Rob isn't it? It's crucial that you get to grips with the importance of what is going on here. On behalf of WHIP, I am working on the reconstruction of a trench at Ypres during World War One to beef up our celebration of Armed Forces Day next week. I've arranged for some young military cadets from the school up the road to patrol along the duckboards during the event and they'll demonstrate the conditions that our brave boys had to contend with when they were under fire. This is all official - approved by senior councillors and your Chief Executive - and I'm very pleased with the progress that's been made so far to realise my vision.'

When Rob failed to be moved by Charles's passionate defence of his harebrained scheme, Cllr Horsfield reverted to his familiar acid tones,

'Now pay attention to what I have to say, er Rob. I expect - no I actually demand - that you'll be suited and booted next week to honour the sacrifices that the military made for pen pushers like you and your pals in the Council offices. Oh, and be a good chap and instruct the media to give this event top coverage will you?'

Rob was peeved that he had not been warned about the ridiculous escapade earlier, especially since a sanctimonious cretin like Horsfield obviously wanted to generate some interest in media circles. However, putting aside the bad vibes of their initial verbal joust, he faked a cheesy grin and told the councillor that he would do his best to generate some publicity when he met up with the local reporters who would be attending the Planning Committee meeting later in the day.

Rob then beat a hasty retreat from the scene of his near accident, and headed straight for the portacabin occupied by Stanley Seymour, the WDC Head of Maintenance, to inform him that Woldshire's most gormless politician was supervising the tearing up of a pristine grass verge with the apparent approval of Viv Bushby. He knew from experience that Stan, a former RAF man, was not exactly Horsfield's biggest fan and often called him the *weekend toy soldier*.

As expected, Stan cursed under his breath after Rob had briefed him on what was going on, and he reluctantly set about rejigging his daily schedule of tasks so that the site could be secured promptly and the Health and Safety Executive informed, with a view to sending someone over to inspect the works when they were completed,

'That's all I needed today, Rob - another soddin' job to add to my list of priority stuff. I can't stand that bloody WHIP amateur! He ought to swap places with me for a day to see what real work is like rather than making his idle threats about chucking boat people overboard or bringing back the death penalty. What a feckin' arsewipe!'

Chapter X

Racist rage revealed

Rob's next port of call was the office of the Council's Chief Legal Advisor, Meera Chopra, a demure middle aged woman of Asian descent who was always very amenable in her dealings with him. She was eating lunch at her desk when Rob ambled into the room and, although he offered to return later, she pressed him to join her, insisting that she had more than enough for two. He was tempted to decline her kind offer out of politeness when he suddenly realised - to his pleasant surprise - that his appetite had returned with a vengeance, and he was ravenous. The delicious smell of home made samosas was wafting up his nostrils, and the effects of his hangover were finally dissipating, so he gave in without much resistance.

While they both tucked into Meera's warm and satisfying treats, Rob started to tell her about the shenanigans going on directly outside the building. As he regaled her with a blow by blow account of his contretemps with Cllr Horsfield, Meera nodded sagely and raised her eyebrows - but Rob noticed that she said very little during pauses in his commentary. He knew that she was an arch critic of Woldshire's leading white supremacist and was normally keen to ridicule his antics when the chance arose. The least he expected from her would have been a query regarding the legality and safety of what old *Horseface* was up to. Rob finally broke off his monologue and asked her why she was so unresponsive.

Meera turned in her chair, looked him in the eye and said gravely,

'Rob, I've come to realise that the man is poison. He's the embodiment of everything that is going wrong in this country, so I'm trying to ignore his existence and hope that he stays away from me. Otherwise I don't think I'll retain my sanity.'

64

Rob was somewhat taken aback by her defeatist tone and, after some prompting, Meera explained more about where she was coming from,

'Let me tell you some things about myself that you may not know. My maternal grandparents left Uganda in 1972 when Idi Amin gave Asian residents ninety days to get out.'

'Ninety days!'

'Yes, the bastard couldn't wait to get rid of our people. Thankfully, this country took them both in, and they worked their fingers to the bone to justify their value to the UK. They saved money to buy a convenience store in town and my mother - their only child - worked there from when she was a youngster. Eventually, she took over running the shop when my grandparents retired. By then, she and my Dad had been wed and, you know, they made a really great team, especially when you consider that it was an arranged marriage so they didn't have much of a say in it. If anything, they put in even longer hours in the store than my grandparents had, and they also found the time to raise a family - me and my two older brothers.'

'Well, that's marvellous, Meera. I'm sure that you're really proud of everything they have achieved.'

'I am - but I'm even more impressed by the desire my parents showed to ensure that life would be good for me and my brothers. They were determined to give us a good start in life and always insisted that we must do our best in school - and there would have been fireworks coming out of their ears if we'd messed up like some of the other kids. Getting a good education for all of us was their holy grail and that's probably why we did so well academically. Raj is a senior consultant in the NHS now, Ronan is a Head teacher and I went down the legal route and ended up here. When I gained a first in law at Oxford they both could have jumped somersaults over the moon.'

'I'm not surprised - you've all done really well by the sound of it.'

'That may be so, but there's always been a downside to our family's success. From their earliest days in the UK, my grandparents had to deal with hostile attitudes when a certain type of white person came into their shop. My Mum and Dad also got the same sort of abuse at times but things seemed to be improving over the years, especially when my brothers and I came into the world as second generation Brits. But now things have become a lot worse again.'

'Why is that then Meera?'

'That ridiculous Brexit referendum in 2016 - that's why. I realise that lots of people voted to leave the EU because they felt we lacked independence on sovereignty issues, but there's also a fair number of racists out there who saw that vote as a free pass to crawl out from under their rocks and flaunt their hideous xenophobia.'

'You mean people like Horsfield and his chums in the Woldwater Home Independence Party?'

'In a nutshell! They might call themselves patriots and look perfectly respectable but I know for a fact that the real reason they call themselves WHIP is because it stands for *We Hate Indians and Pakistanis.'*

'Ah - that makes a lot of sense now that you say it.'

'But they will always deny it won't they? You can't prove anything and they're very cunning when they want to be. Anyway, I thought that their bigotry wouldn't intrude too much on my work here at the Council and I guess that quietly taking the mickey out of them now and then was my way of dealing with their vile existence. But the other day, I'm convinced that they set up one of their brainless neanderthals to shake me up.'

'They went to all that trouble?'

'I reckon. A cheeky young chap, who I'd never heard from before, called me and asked for an appointment to discuss a legal matter of high importance that was relevant to the well being of the Council. Well, I was on my guard a bit but I stupidly agreed to meet him last Tuesday and he arrived at the reception desk and waited for me there. I should have known he was trouble as soon as I was going down the stairs to greet him because he didn't look very pleased to see me. When I finally approached him he refused to shake my hand and then he shouted at the top of his voice that he wanted to discuss his business with *a proper white lawyer and not some jumped up chapati muncher fresh off a boat* - and then he just flounced off.'

'That's awful. What a plonker! But how do you really know for sure that WHIP was behind this?'

'Well, it seems rather fishy that Cllr Horsfield just happened to be in the foyer at that very moment - and when I glanced across at him when that nutter was bawling me out, old *Horseface* looked like the cat that had got the cream. And, here's the clincher... just before I turned around to go upstairs - I was nearly in tears by then, mind you - he called me across and whispered in my ear that people like me should realise that times have changed and I should piss off back to my homeland if I knew what was good for me and the rest of my family.'

'Bloody hell - have you reported any of this?'

'What's the point? Normally people come to me about this sort of stuff and I take action if necessary. I'm not used to being the offended party. Anyway, he would just come out with some crap about his trying to console me after that guy gave me a hard time, and he'll say that I must have misheard him.'

She continued,

'I forgot to mention that Cllr Sharkey was milling around as well - another strange coincidence - and he was smiling sweetly all the time that *Horseface* was making his filthy threats so everybody in reception thought that his mate from WHIP was acting like a knight in shining bloody armour. But there's no mistaking that Horsfield has it in for me, Rob, and I'll have to watch my step with him in future. And I daresay the Tories won't lift a finger to do anything about it either. So that's why I'm not bothered about him digging the odd hole here and there - he can do what the hell he likes as far as I'm concerned, provided he leaves me alone. Stan can sort it all out on the health and safety side - he's a white male and that means *Horseface* won't make so much of a fuss if there's any hassle.'

Rob was enraged that Meera had been cowed into submission, but she told him to cool down and diverted the conversation towards the matter she had wanted to discuss when she called him earlier that day. She began to explain how a council employee who was a Civil Enforcement Officer - the posh term for Traffic Warden - was in a spot of bother,

'It all seemed quite straightforward at first, Rob. The CEO noticed that a parked car had gone well over the limit in a 30 minute parking zone and he issued a Penalty Charge Notice. We always insist that our CEOs take photos to show the location and the time when the offence was committed, and that's where this problem starts. It turns out that there was a young child in the car when the photo was taken and now the driver - her father - is claiming that the CEO took a snapshot of his daughter without permission.'

'So it's ok to leave your little darling alone in a parked vehicle while you do some shopping, but you have every right to go bananas if someone allegedly takes a photo of the car and she happens to be caught on camera?'

'Well, he reckons that his wife was in the rear seat with the kid at the time - but he's probably lying his backside off about that. To be honest, when you look at the photo you can't really see whether there is anyone at all inside the car - there's a sort of dark blobby image and the father swears you can make out the face of his child if you blow it up. And this is where you come in, Rob - he's threatened to go to the press, claiming that the traffic warden is some sort of paedophile. As you can imagine, our guy is on sick leave at the moment because of this fiasco, and he's stressed up to his eyeballs.'

'How about just letting off the motorist by cancelling the fine? Wouldn't that be enough to shut him up and put this all to bed?'

'Oh, we've gone well beyond that, Rob. He's claiming compensation for the upset caused to him and his wife, and he's demanded an apology from the Chief Exec as well. And the cherry on the cake is that he also wants us to dismiss the traffic warden - it's Bert Robson and he's been with the Council for thirty odd years.'

'I know old Bert. He's been around the block a bit but he's as good as gold.'

'Between you and me, his name is probably high on the list of staff cuts that we're drawing up. We have to make savings, as you know, and he's racked up enough years to qualify for a generous redundancy package. It won't be quite so peachy for him if we have to dismiss him for a misdemeanour and he needs to find another job, but I think we can still swing this so that he leaves us with a clean record. We just need you to keep the media sweet if the driver carries out his threat and goes to them about the sex offence allegations. Can you convince them that he's way out of order?'

'I'll see what I can do. I'm owed a big favour by the editor at The Examiner because they cocked up a report about a nuisance case the other week. I tipped them off when I noticed that their online story had misidentified the culprit and managed to stop them making the same mistake in their print version. By the way, you're sure that this parking spat is just this guy's word against ours?'

'Definitely. We know he's trying it on but we'll drop the penalty charge as promised. He can whistle for an apology from the Chief Exec and if he approaches the local media with such a grainy photo we should be home and dry, provided they tell him where to get off. We've checked and he doesn't seem to have a social media account so we'll keep our fingers crossed that he runs out of steam.'

'I'll ring around when I get back and try to put the mockers on this one. The chances are that he won't even approach the press, but I'll forewarn them that a chancer might be trying his luck.'

'Thanks, Rob. And not a word to anyone about the possible redundancy for Bert eh?'

'My lips are sealed'.

Chapter XI

Drilling down

When late afternoon came around, Rob felt completely drained. He could sense his mental faculties going into meltdown again, having spent a long while chatting up his local media contacts. Nevertheless, he was happy with the end result because he was quietly confident that he had quashed any potential news stories that might have been generated by paedo traffic warden allegations.

He was relieved that he had managed to conduct such a clean fight during his discussions, avoiding references to the strategic weapon he held in reserve - the 'hard copy' nuclear button. With sales of

71

newspapers continuing to dwindle, the regional media had come to regard published notices income as a financial life support machine. The main contributors to the coffers were local authorities across the country who were duty bound to alert residents about certain issues (such as planning notices and election information) in print. This meant that Councils were required to fork out considerable sums for the publication of the information in hard copy format. For this reason, proprietors in the regional news sector lobbied Westminster frequently to ensure that the outmoded means of compliance was retained, even though it made a lot of sense to switch completely to a much cheaper electronic means of communication.

Most editors, including Al Miron at The Woldshire Examiner, were acutely aware that the hard copy requirements might be watered down considerably if they were to bite the hand that fed them over much, and he tended to be quite forward-leaning in his dealings with Council's comms office. When Rob very occasionally rang asking him to take a more lenient line on a dubious issue, or perhaps even drop coverage of an iffy story altogether, Al was sometimes willing to give ground provided the request seemed reasonable.

In this instance, once Rob had explained the background to the dodgy parking fine story, Al didn't need much persuading to lose the scent,

'So he went well over the limit on his time and the warden took a photo of the car in situ as was his normal practice?'

'Yes - it was a slam dunk parking offence. The motorist was thirty minutes over.'

'And now he's claiming that your guy is a kiddy fiddler on the basis of a piss poor photo that allegedly shows his daughter sitting in the back of the car?'

'Yes but it might as well be a snapshot of the Pope or the second coming of Elvis Presley given the crap definition.'

'Well, I think we can probably let that one go if it arises, Rob, especially since you gave our guys a heads up the other day about our misidentification of the chap playing the loud music in Bellamy Gardens. I still don't know how we managed to name the complainant as the perpetrator but I don't think he would have been too happy to see our cock-up in print.'

Rob had a similarly successful conversation with Al's counterpart at the Gazette and, ordinarily, he would have reflected happily on a job well done and retired to the pub for a celebration pint or two at the end of a gruelling day. But he was acutely aware that the Planning Committee meeting at Reilly Road was due to begin at four thirty and he had to gird his loins for a grim three hour session in the Chamber. At that moment he felt deeply resentful towards Ozzie who didn't need to stay and had packed up early to play in a five a side football tournament at the Woldchester Leisure Centre.

Before his junior colleague left for the day, Rob had asked him to attend a meeting with the ageing Council Chairman, Cllr Keith Wharton, who was planning a grand ball to support his two official charities - one providing short break holidays for single parent families and the other funding a helpline for kids in danger of self harm. Rob subsequently learned that Ozzie had persuaded the old codger to maximise the amount of money going to his two good

73

causes by opting for a cheaper live band than his original choice. And so it came to pass that *Rockin' All Over the Wold* were booked for the gig at a special discounted price. Unbeknown to Cllr Wharton, the young charmer actually fronted the band, and his mate Gibbo played bass guitar! The young lad might be a bit of a pain at times but Rob had to confess that he was a colourful character in an environment where people with that brand of chutzpah were few and far between.

After bolting down a tired looking tuna mayo sandwich and the last doughnut from the staff canteen, Rob ventured outside again to take a much needed break before the evening meeting started. The sun which had greeted his earlier foray out of doors had disappeared from view, and there was a faint drizzle in the air as he made his way across to the Chamber's public entrance.

This time he was ready for the hazardous trench awaiting him, and he was gratified to see that Stan Seymour had sealed it off very competently with an abundance of barriers. For good measure, the maintenance man had also posted a copious amount of large print notices about the danger and had fashioned a pedestrian walkway to negotiate the patches of mud strewn across the car park. Rob had spent a good while cleaning up after his earlier encounter with the hole in the ground, and he was grateful that his shoes and trousers would remain reasonably clean and tidy for the forthcoming meeting.

The workmen had finished for the day and the abandoned plant machinery indicated that the excavation was still incomplete. That is why Rob could hardly believe his eyes when he glimpsed down and made out a handful of figures who had actually descended into the trench via a couple of ladders. Unless he was mistaken, they appeared to be preparing for military drills below ground. Rob's suspicions were confimed when he became aware that the indomitable Cllr Horsfield was also gazing down at them from the surface. The cretin, who had now abandoned his overalls but was still wearing his silly hard hat, caught sight of Rob and strutted towards him like a Sergeant Major on steroids,

'Ah, just the man I need to speak to. As you can see, we now have six volunteer students in place to practise the reenactment of the World War I experience. These cadets will be doing drills for real when we honour our Armed Forces next week, but I thought a dummy run would make sure that the press have a heads up when they arrive for this evening's meeting. The youngsters will be staying here for about an hour. so I assume there'll be plenty of time for you to organise a media photo shoot eh?'

'Hang on a minute, are you sure those kids should be down in that hole before there's been an official safety inspection? Stan told me that he's arranged for one tomorrow so it's not really too long to wait is it?.'

'What? And miss out on my best chance of a media opportunity to promote the big event? Come on, laddie. What sort of a comms person are you? You've got to seize the day in my book. Surely *I* shouldn't have to tell *you* that. Anyway, tell me what real harm we're doing, eh?'

At that moment, a small Fiat drove up and Rob was distracted when he saw Sandy Staveley alighting. She glanced around and then made her way towards them with a stern look on her face. Cllr Horsfield seemed to be expecting her and beamed a smile of welcome,

75

'Ah, you must be Ms Staveley from Woodchester School. Listen Rob, this young lady has kindly volunteered to organise the drill while I take my seat on the Planning Committee. I don't think you know each other, but I'm sure that you can get acquainted and work together to fill in for me if the media have any questions during my absence. Look, I've run off some leaflets that might help.'

As soon as Horsfield left the scene, Rob turned to Sandy and could hardly contain himself,

'How on earth did you end up with this absolutely ridiculous gig, Sand? '

'Don't get me started, Rob. It was bad enough getting the parents to agree to a stupid after-school activity at short notice, especially since no sane person in the staff room wanted anything to do with this fool's errand whatsoever. Charles Horsfield is one of the governors so the Head had little choice in kowtowing, and we all resorted to drawing straws in the staff room for this crap extra duty. Guess who drew the wee short one? Now then, what the hell am I supposed to do and how soon can I get away from here?'

Rob saw a chance to do the teacher a massive favour while boosting his chances of a night out with her,

'Look, I'll wait around for the reporters to arrive and I'll try and persuade them to take some shots of the cadets. That will give you a chance to hand them the leaflets explaining what's being planned - and then you can all toddle off home .'

'Gosh - that would be great, Rob. I'll really owe you if you can make that work.'

'So you might fancy an evening out after all?'

'Okay. Yes, it's a deal if you can spring me out of this ordeal in a hurry. Just name a date or two and I'll work around it - provided you can get me out of here asap. I need to get back home to mark some assignments that I promised to hand back tomorrow.'

Rob nodded assuredly and hung around with Sandy while waiting for the journalists to arrive. He enjoyed chatting with her about the range of food served up by his favourite Chinese restaurant but his mood changed when he saw a mini bus arrive in the car park at speed, driven by the redoubtable Cllr Ric Sharkey. The doors opened and a group of mostly elderly people dismounted. They were all carrying placards and organised themselves quickly into a small protest group just outside the Chamber entrance. Rob didn't know what exactly was going on, but the presence of *The Shark* suggested that it wasn't anything promising.

As the demonstrators began chanting slogans, Rob peered at the handwritten messages being held aloft on the placards and it became clear why the bus travellers were not happy campers. One was waving a sign that exhorted the Council to *Keep Workshy Scroungers out of our Village*, while another proclaimed that they welcomed *Houses for the needy - not the Greedy*. The message on the largest banner was very forthright - *Little Chipping for hardworking families? - Yes! Big houses for lazy bastards - No!!'* Perhaps the most offensive one of the lot opined that *Scumbags who breed like rabbits should live in hutches!*

When Rob tried to approach the noisy protestors, who were chorusing *SOS. SOS. Save us from this Planning Mess!* Cllr Sharkey intercepted him and observed casually,

'Good. to see democracy in action isn't it Rob? These good people have come down from Little Chipping to try and right a wrong by sending out a cry of help of sorts. I guess that the sparks will be flying soon when the planning application for affordable homes in their village comes up for discussion.'

Rob faked a grin and responded,

'Yes, it's always healthy to see the public taking an interest in our meetings at WDC - but some of these guys look like they're straight out of *Rentacrowd*. It seems a bit odd that you chauffeured them down here, especially since most residents in Little Chipping can easily afford the odd Merc or BMW. Are you sure these protesters are for real, Cllr Sharkey - or are they assorted odds and sods moonlighting to earn a few bob on the side?'

Ric laughed off what he described as a ludicrous accusation and wagged his finger at Rob in an admonitory fashion. In actual fact, the rogue Councillor had slipped a few *ringers* from Tory Party HQ into the mix to boost the numbers, but he was confident that he had also crammed enough bonafide locals on to the bus to support his assertion, so he went on the offensive,

'I think you ought to mind your tongue before you start making unfounded allegations, Rob - these good people are concerned residents who heard about a lousy planning proposal and they're standing up for their right to oppose it. And if Jim Harvey and his merry band of fools at County Hall got their act together and laid on better public transport facilities, they all could have come to the meeting using a scheduled bus service instead of me having to do the business. Anyway, I'm not sure why you're poking your nose in - I expect the press won't need you sniffing around to figure out that a load of undesirables are being shunted into a peaceful village - so if you'll excuse me, I have bigger buns to bake.'

Rob felt like he'd been slapped across the buttocks with a wet towel. Just by reading the messages on the placards, he was beginning to realise the dire consequences of the Council relocating Karen Craig, Fred Clark and thirteen kids to Little Chipping on the Wold. He was angry that the Leader of the Coalition hadn't briefed him in advance about this delicate matter, and he was downright astonished that they had been trying to sweep it under the carpet in the hope that nobody would notice!

Rob also blamed himself and his alcohol-fuddled brain for not working out the implications of building one house much bigger than the others in a small village dominated by middle class families. He braced himself for more unpalatable details coming to light when the debate got underway and feared that events might turn very ugly later on.

As the mob prepared to ascend into the Chamber, Rob noticed a couple of familiar reporters - Tom Irwin from the Examiner and the Gazette's Lena Montgomery - also making their way up the steps to the meeting. They had both stopped in their tracks en route to take a few photos of the protest and had also been eager to question Cllr Sharkey about the underlying reason. Obviously, *The Shark* had beenhappy to provide them with some scurrilous background information about the *tin-eared* administration's flawed affordable housing plans.

In their haste to glean details of the Little Chipping fiasco, the reporters had largely ignored the teenagers marching up and down the trench, despite Sandy and Rob's best efforts to invite their attention. Rob resorted to yelling at the hacks to wander over just before they entered the Chamber, and was dismayed when Tom declared that youngsters should find better things to do with their time after school hours. Lena pitched in with her observation that the wartime memorial activity was a *crap idea that ought to be strangled at birth*.

Clutching at straws, Rob pleaded to Sandy,

'Look, er, Sand, how about if you keep them drilling for a while and I'll chat to Tom and Lena upstairs to see if I can get them to come down and have a word with you after the first agenda item? Lena always trots down for a fag break so I could be pushing at an open door once I've softened her up. I'll take some leaflets to try and get them both a bit more interested. Maybe I can rope in *Horseface* as well to swing things your way.'

If looks could kill, Sandy's icy glare aimed at Rob would have landed him in A&E, but she agreed reluctantly to hang around for a while longer and steeled herself for a further bout of ennui.

Chapter XII

Protest pandemonium

The Planning Committee meeting got underway at four thirty on the dot and, just in the nick of time, Rob managed to gain his usual position in the Chamber, alongside the desk reserved for the press.

80

This enabled him to provide any assistance required by the media representatives, including names and roles of the speakers when they popped up to say their piece.

The protestors were the only members of the public seated in the gallery and were no doubt pleased to note that the affordable housing application in Little Chipping was first up on the agenda.

The Chair of the Planning Committee, Cllr Don Hilley, banged his gavel to start the proceedings and was looking rather apprehensive, probably because he had seen the messages on the placards when he had parked his Audi. He'd also clocked the troublesome Cllr Sharkey in their midst and dreaded that the mischievous councillor was going to be a thorn in his flesh before the meeting concluded. He adjusted the volume button on his microphone nervously and announced the first matter for consideration.

At first, the mood in the room was quite orderly as the Chief Planning Officer briefed the Committee on the proposed development at Little Chipping. This involved the use of a Powerpoint display which showed an artist's impression of the houses, as well as photos and diagrams of the relevant boundaries, road links, sewage disposal systems and other otiose miscellanies.

The atmosphere changed markedly when the CPO finished his spiel and members of the committee were invited to comment. *The Shark's* protege, Cllr Lesley Ashurst, was the first out of the blocks,

"This is an admirable project in principle and I can confirm that the Conservative party endorses the concept one hundred and ten percent. But if you delve beneath the surface gloss, there's an abomination here that needs to be highlighted. While it's true that several deserving residents will be accommodated in much needed new build affordable family homes - thanks to the Netherwold Vale Housing Association - I must question why a dwelling that amounts to a mansion is being constructed for one particular family. And this is no ordinary family, my friends. As far as I know, they are NOT in paid work, they rely on a WIDE range of benefits at the taxpayer's expense, they DISTURB other residents continuously in their current accommodation, they DON'T contribute to the wellbeing of their community - and there are THIRTEEN of them all under one roof.'

Lesley paused her rant expertly, allowing a breathing space for supporters in the gallery to cheer and clap. When Cllr Hilley finally brought them to order, she added more fuel to the fire,

'In this day and age when resources are scarce and money is tight, how can we put up with this sort of reckless spending in our District? I realise that something needs to be done about these people because they are housed in unsuitable accommodation at the moment - but the answer is NOT to use them as a wrecking ball to disturb the peace somewhere else. Surely Social Services can step in and sort them out? If they can't be housed in more modest accommodation, then there must be ways and means to split them into more manageable family units.'

At this point, there was a crescendo of applause and, once the noise had died down, the Tory tyro continued in the same vein,

'I assume there is nobody here from the Meadow Estate in East Woldchester where this family is currently living? No? Not a soul? Well, is anyone surprised? There you have it - not a single neighbour will come here today and speak up for them. And the reason why is obvious; they will all be extremely glad to see the back of them. I expect they're hoping that our Committee will nod through this application so that they can be rid of this wretched family once and for all. Fortunately, many of the good folk of Little Chipping have turned up this evening to oppose this solution, and are waiting eagerly to see justice done. And that is why I cannot support this application today.'

As she concluded, Rob noticed that Lena and Tom were typing notes on their laptops at breakneck speed, and hadn't even glanced at the World War I enactment leaflets that he had placed prominently on their desk. Meanwhile, the protestors in the Chamber had to be tamped down yet again because they had unfurled a new banner that declared *Little Chipping SOS = Sod Off Scumbags.*

The next committee member to comment on the application was Cllr Horsfield who rose from his seat to pitch in his two pennorth,

'I agree entirely with my colleague Cllr Ashurst. It's clear that the administration here is trying to pull the wool over our eyes and they've been sussed. This is the first I've heard of this skullduggery and I for one will be rejecting this application when it comes to the vote. It makes me furious that young upstanding citizens of the future are taking part in a practice drill outside as they prepare to honour our Armed Forces in a few days from now and - at the same time - we're gathering here to consider rewarding benefit scroungers for doing nothing to justify their scandalous lifestyle.'

He sat down to raucous cheers and Rob noticed that Cllr Sharkey was nodding vigorously and giving his WHIP colleague the thumbs up sign. When the hullabaloo died down again, the Coalition stalwart Cllr Kelvin Kettleborough was given permission to speak.

He was revving up to refute the SOS allegations when one of the protestors shouted,

'Go back to sleep you old bugger, that's your specialist skill, according to the Internet. We've all seen the memes on social media, you dozy sod!'

Cllr Kettleborough ignored the jibe and launched forth to defend the actions of the Coalition,

'What I'm hearing this evening is absolutely preposterous. Cllr Ashurst and Cllr Horsfield are ignoring the fact that a good number of families are being given a wonderful chance to rent, buy or part-buy their own homes in one of the prettiest villages in the district. Despite the hot air circulating around this Chamber, I can say hand on heart that we're NOT building a luxury mansion to accommodate a specific client. What we're doing here is creating a basic house with enough bedrooms to allow them to live together as a unit. Yes,I admit that it's big in comparison with a normal home, but this new build represents a considerable cost saving for the Council in comparison with what we're currently paying out in housing subsidies to meet the needs of the family.'

Sensing that he might be getting through to his audience, he continued,

'At present, they live in two semis with a hole knocked through the wall and it's little wonder that they find it difficult to function well. And what on earth is the point of splitting them up? The costs would rocket and I dread to think of the hardship we might cause. We're talking about human beings here, some of whom are just babes in arms - they're NOT animals.'

As he paused again. someone shouted,

'Well they certainly behave like animals - why does anyone need so many kids for God's sake?'

Cllr Kettleborough responded

'What gives anyone the right to pass judgement on these people? I'm reminded of the biblical passage about *he who throws the first stone*. The last time I looked, I don't remember that it was against the law to have a large family. You say that they've caused a nuisance in their neighbourhood - well, we have ways and means of dealing with that sort of behaviour if and when it occurs, and we have no record of any official complaints made to the Council about this family.'

Another protester interrupted,

'That's because they probably threaten people who might dob them in, Mr Councillor. They're a walking nightmare, and you know it.'

Cllr Kettleborough sidestepped the interjection, and ploughed on,

'Innuendo and gossip is being used to undermine a planning application worthy of our unanimous approval. In fact, I wouldn't be surprised if this is all a pretext to prevent the construction of affordable homes in one of our more select locations. *Not in my backyard* is a phrase that springs to mind in this instance.'

He was winding up to deliver a vicious verbal assault on the privileged classes when the Chamber door swung open suddenly and a small scruffy looking girl ran into the room, crying out at the top of her voice,

'My Mum says that everyone should leave now because there's a lot of er like water outside in the car park - and she says that it's bleedin' dangerous!'

Chapter XIII

Briefs encounter

About ten minutes before the little girl's surprise intervention in the events within the Chamber, Sandy had almost lost the will to live. The Combined Cadet Force kids were tired of the novelty of marching up and down in a trench and a shower of light rain was turning into a chilly downpour. She was dreading the two hours worth of assignment marking that was waiting for her at home and that grim prospect finally persuaded her to wind things up, regardless of the chance of gaining some press coverage should the cadets hang around for a while longer.

She was at the point of ordering everyone to pack up when she was distracted by the noise of gears grating as a dilapidated VW camper van limped into the Reilly Road car park. When the vehicle shuddered to a halt, the doors opened and a couple of ageing hippy types alighted, accompanied by several children of varying ages. Sandy wasn't aware at first that she was witnessing the arrival of the infamous Karen Craig and Fred Clark, along with several of their children.

The two adults approached Sandy and asked for directions to the Council Chamber.

On first acquaintance, they exuded an air of other worldliness that she found rather weird. Karen looked to be in her forties and had very long hair that hid most of her elfin face, although it was still clear that she was fond of piercings. She was wearing a kaftan overlaid with an old Barbour jacket which was about two sizes too large for her delicate frame. In comparison, Fred was a giant of a man with close cropped hair, and Sandy guessed that he was probably about the same age as his partner. He was wearing well for a middle aged guy, and could have passed muster as a *shabby chic* aficionado dressed in his black tee shirt and shorts. His arms were covered in lurid tattoos that were quite off putting in Sandy's opinon, but she was captivated by his genial smile and courteous attitude.

They didn't question why she was standing guard over a group of teenagers in uniform, and she wasn't inclined to enlighten them in her rush to get home. She told them where the meeting was taking place and was quite relieved when they parted company with her and she could get on with bringing the drill to a close.

Just as the Craig/Clark family members were making their way up the steps to the planning meeting, they were brought to a halt by an ear-piercing shriek that arose from the trench. As if by magic, a jet of water shot about twenty feet into the air at high velocity. Sandy 's first reaction was to stare in wonder at the instant fountain that had appeared out of nowhere, and it took her a few seconds to realise that an extremely hazardous situation was developing. The howling continued as the earthworks filled up at a rate of knots and young lives were suddenly at risk.

Fred and Karen turned around to take in the horrific scene unfolding below them and they could hardly believe their eyes.

Within about ten seconds, it looked like the trench had filled to the brim with water which was now spilling over into the car park. Sandy gathered her wits quickly and did her best to usher the cadets away from danger, but a quick head count revealed that two of the students in her charge were trapped in the dugout - hence the yells of terror emanating from there.

Although Fred looked rather slovenly to the casual observer, years spent working on construction sites and oil rigs had toughened him up considerably. He knew instinctively that it was down to him to avert a potential tragedy, and he hastily instructed Karen to phone the emergency services while he rushed down the stairs . The other members of his family were urged to make their way to Sandy to help her find a safe place for her charges. While he was barking out his instructions, Fred stripped to his underwear, and clambered over a barricade before plunging into the murky waters of the trench in search of the two missing kids.

In an instant, he was completely submerged under the raging surface which now resembled a large cauldron on the boil. Shortly afterwards, the big man resurfaced holding a cold and frightened young lad in his arms and passed him across the barrier to Karen, who had retrieved a couple of dog blankets from the van to provide essential warmth. Fred also glimpsed his eldest child rushing forward with a hot drink for the young lad - sweetened tea from a flask in the camper van.

He sprinted back to the trench and jumped in again feet first. This time around, he remained under the surface for what seemed like a frustratingly long time which caused Karen and Sandy to fear for the worst. They huddled together at the barrier and exchanged anxious looks when there was no sign of progress. Small talk was out of the question, and both women stared at the trench in silence, oblivious to the fact that filthy floodwater had spilled across the car park and was now swirling around their knees.

Eventually, to their joint relief, Fred came into view again, this time cradling the body of a small uniformed girl. Karen and Sandy were both sick with fear when they observed the listless form being deposited on the ground, but Fred hauled himself over the edge of the trench like a whirling dervish and began to administer cardiopulmonary resuscitation for all he was worth.

Both women were dumbstruck as Fred worked furiously to coax some life into the poor little mite. Sandy never thought of herself as a religious person but she recited a little prayer from her junior school days in her head to ward off her sense of helplessness as the seconds ticked away and the cause seemed lost. Karen preferred to cross her fingers, and kept looking up at the sky like she was expecting some kind of divine intervention. She was obviously relieved that Fred was still in one piece, but she wondered how the mother of the girl would react if she never saw her child alive again. Clutching a blanket that was intended for wrapping around the student to warm her up, she wondered if it would soon be serving as a shroud instead.

When it seemed like all hope was gone, Fred detected a trickle of water coming out of the girl's mouth and nostrils, and then her eyes started to flicker into life. Sandy and Karen could hardly believe what was happening and tears started to stream down their faces. The two women, who had been complete strangers a few minutes earlier, embraced tightly when it dawned on them that Fred had brought the girl back to life. After swaddling her in the blanket, they both took off their coats to give the little mite some extra warmth.

Fred was grinning from ear to ear and said to Karen,

'Will you look at that, love! I thought she was a goner, but I just kept pumping away - and, by God, it did the trick! I'm well chuffed with that, so I am.'

Karen threw herself into his arms and kissed him full on the lips but he drew back from her clinch quickly because he still sensed more danger ahead, and told her to save her ardour for later,

'Look at all the water - it's swamping the car park now! Listen love, get the little 'un to go up to the Chamber and tell everyone to retrieve their cars before they're washed away.'

Turning to Sandy, he queried whether the other students were out of harm's way. She confirmed that they were all present and correct, grouped together on the steps near the Chamber and well above the water level.

Fred still wasn't at ease and asked Sandy,

'What's below that ridge where the water's dropping down? Is it safe?'

She couldn't really help much and muttered,

'Er, I don't know for sure but - oh my goodness - I think it might be sheltered housing.'

On hearing this news, Fred leapt into action once again,

'Oh, balls and bounce the buggers! We'd better get down there smartish before we have another near disaster on our hands!'

Despite being soaked to the skin and wearing only his underwear, Fred raced down the hill beyond the car park and started knocking loudly on doors to alert residents that they must evacuate their houses urgently. Some of his children accompanied him to help some of the elderly folk out of their homes and they began leading them to the safety of higher ground.

While this was happening, the attendees from the Planning Committee meeting had been alerted and were emerging from the building to take in the surreal new landscape. All the safety barriers had now been washed away, and a small lake had appeared where there should have been a car park, making it rather tricky to retrieve any vehicles.

Just as the Chamber was emptying, three fire engines appeared at speed, shortly followed by two ambulances, three police cars and a couple of vans from the regional water company. The emergency services personnel took charge of the situation swiftly and the crowd was contained on a terrace outside the building until they could bring the situation under control. While this was going on, the Chief Fire Officer made her way towards a mud-streaked savage looking man clad in underpants and vest who appeared from beyond a grassy ridge leading a pack of senior residents, some of whom were supported by children.

It soon became clear to the senior *Blue Light* Officer that Fred had saved the day, and he received a few pats on the back from her when he was asked to stand down from his unexpected role and join the others on the stairs.

Meanwhile, several council officers who had been in attendance at the Planning Committee meeting had already initiated the emergency response procedures that they practised on a regular basis. As soon as he realised the potential impact of the flooding, WDC's de facto coordinator - the Chief Planning Officer - began calling out responders in line with a rota that he always carried with him. He knew that his council colleagues would be rushing to convert the nearby leisure centre into a rest centre and he alerted the Chief Fire Officer that the Council was preparing to play its part in resolving the crisis.

The *blue light* personnel worked tirelessly to get things on an even keel at the scene of the flood, and watching them in action was like poetry in motion. Their first priority was activating powerful pumps to drain the bulk of the surface water into the nearby canal and away from danger. This paved the way for the engineers from the water company to explore the source of the leak, and they rapidly located a stopcock in the building to reduce the flow to a relative trickle. The young female cadet who had been trapped in the trench was whisked away in an ambulance and, the car park water level soon dropped markedly and it was beginning to look more navigable again, despite being strewn with silt and rubble.

When she was satisfied that it was safe to proceed, the Chief Fire Officer gave the go ahead for the public to descend the steps from the Chamber, making sure that the Council's emergency responders - who had all been issued with high visibility tabards - were on hand to guide them down the steps. By this time, an additional group of WDC volunteers had arrived at the Council headquarters, and were ready and waiting in their cars to ferry people across town to the newly created rest centre. Social media enthusiasts had already picked up on the events at Reilly Road and a small crowd began to gather in the neighbourhood, some of whom were shamefully gleaning as many lurid details as possible for their Facebook accounts.

Sharp eyed observers would have spied Cllr Sharkey returning to inspect his mini bus. He was surprised that the engine was still turning when he pressed the ignition switch and thanked the heavens that the engine was higher above ground in contrast to the cars around him that were all out of action.

He offered to return the group of protestors to their homes and most of them jumped at the chance rather than being ferried to the Leisure Centre for the evening. Their banners had been abandoned in the Chamber and they weren't in a hurry to retrieve them. Once they were all aboard the bus, Sharkey gunned the motor and they sped off at a rate of knots. A haggard looking Cllr Lesley Ashurst bade them farewell and then set off for her apartment on foot, wondering when her Fiat 500 would be roadworthy again.

Chapter XIV

A change is as good as a rest centre

Ozzie Burton was just finishing his game of five a side football at Woldchester Leisure Centre when the teams were instructed to leave the building quickly because it was required to host an emergency rest centre. Being a member of the Council's response team, he guessed that his services would be required so he made himself known at the reception desk and was told to help set up some tables and chairs.

Within a few minutes, cars started arriving with a collection of old people, youngsters in uniform and various councillors, who were ushered into the main sports hall. What had previously been the venue for Ozzie's kick around was being transformed into a place of safety, complete with a sitting area, several camp beds, blankets, tea and coffee making facilities and a snack bar.

The Chief Executive's PA, Maria Milburn, arrived to supervise the kitchen, and various other council workers reported for duty in response to the cascade briefing rota instigated by the Chief Planning Officer. Before setting off, Maria had informed Viv Bushby about what was going on and advised her to travel down to Woldchester as soon as possible. She noticed Rob approaching the main entrance with a young woman, followed by five teenagers who looked rather bedraggled. Maria waved to him as he walked by but he was deep in conversation with his female companion and didn't see her. Being Rob's ex-wife, Maria had an intuition that Rob was quite besotted with his female companion just by the look on his face. She judged that the woman was definitely Rob's type, and she hoped that he had finally found someone who might be right for him.

Rob and Sandy were pleased to see that the cadets trailing behind them were treating the whole episode like a big adventure. After they entered the building, she held on tightly to the hand of the little guy who had been rescued from the trench and then made sure that he was settled comfortably on a camp bed. Once that was done, she busied herself with a series of phone calls alerting parents that they should come to retrieve their children from the Leisure Centre.

After she had completed that task, Rob perceived that Sandy wilted somewhat and then ran out of steam completely; she sat down for a short break and was a lot more withdrawn in comparison to her usual bouncy self. Rob had made sure that the remaining kids were content, plying them with drinks and crisps while they waited for their lifts home, and he made his way across to Sandy again to enquire whether she was okay.

At that moment, she virtually collapsed against his body, and started to sob uncontrollably. Rob instinctively put his arms around her and was gratified that she let him comfort her in this way. As he held her close to him, he calmly told her to take deep breaths and reflect on the good job that she had done. Sandy continued crying, albeit less heavily, but it was evident that she was far from convinced by his reassurances,

'I'm not so sure about doing a good job, Rob! I nearly lost two kids tonight and I was trusted to look after them. You know, I've always thought that I was pretty damned good when it came to supervising all the brats from school ... but I felt so bloody helpless out there tonight. My biggest test as a guardian and I ..'

Rob sensed that she was bordering on hysteria and tried to soothe her,

'Hang on - stop beating yourself up. You were great tonight - none of this was your fault.'

She still wasn't buying his blandishments,

'Not my fault? Look, I was meant to be in charge and I let them down when they needed my protection. One moment they were playing at being soldiers down in that trench, and the next thing I knew they were being swept away in a flood of water. I mean, don't get me wrong, I was ecstatic when they were rescued, but I still feel like I've failed them big time.'

Rob disagreed completely,

'Hey, Sand, once you get over this you'll realise that there's nothing you could have done any differently. That idiot *Horseface* is the sole reason why those kids were put at risk - it's got nothing to do with you, and it would have have happened to anyone who drew was supervising them. Charles was so hung up on publicising his daft idea that he didn't think through any of the hazards. I'm guessing that one of the diggers must have fractured a pipe below ground so how can you say that you were to blame for any of this?'

While they spoke at length, parents of the teenagers began to enter the hall and were reunited with their offspring. There were tears and laughter as the families came together and details of the event were recalled by the children. One of the mothers approached Sandy and told her that she'd just received an upbeat text message from the parents of the little girl who had been taken to hospital; apparently, she was doing fine and was in good spirits. That good news was like a shot of adrenalin as far as Sandy was concerned, and Rob actually got a smile out of her when he brought her a much needed cup of coffee and a cheese sandwich.

Ordinarily the press would have been excluded from the rest centre, but Tom Irwin and Lena Montgomery were notable exceptions to the rule, as they had been evacuated from the Chamber and were therefore legitimate attendees. Both reporters made the most of their lucky break and soon got down to filing exclusive *on the spot* reports about the incident.

 For obvious reasons, the man of the moment was Fred Clark. Staff from the Leisure Centre had provided him with towels for a hot shower and had then kitted him out in a spare tracksuit. He was now tucking into a bacon sandwich while swigging countless mugs of tea and Karen was hovering dutifully by his side. Their children had found a trampoline in a side room at the rear of the main hall, and were amusing themselves to their heart's content.

Once Fred was replete, Tom and Lena descended on him like hawks and asked him for an account of his brave deeds. Being a man of few words, Fred tended to leave most of the talking to Karen, but the reporters didn't mind because she was a natural storyteller and she brought the whole episode to life. Despite Karen's vivid embellishments, Fred was intent on playing things down when he got a word in edgeways, but Sandy caught sight of him and felt the urge to butt in,

'Whatever you write, guys, please make absolutely sure that you stress that this humble man is a bloody hero. He brought a little girl back to life tonight. I've never seen anything like it in all my born days. It was truly amazing!'

Karen chipped in,

'He's the dog's bollocks, and that's a fact! He's one in a million, our Fred. Did you know that he does all this Zen Buddhism stuff, and he used to disappear for months on end helping people in need around the world? He would just shoot off in the van to places where there'd been all kinds of disasters and then he cooked like shed loads of rice and beans. He ended up in the strangest locations.'

Tom and Lena couldn't believe their luck. They'd happened upon a great back story and encouraged Karen to tell them more,

'Well, he always came back to me and the kids with loads of tales about the people he'd met - but he hasn't been away much since the doc told me I had MS. He's been great helping me cope. I haven't been able to work for a couple of years now, you see, and he's been my rock. The kids are fantastic too and they're all getting me through this.'

This was gold dust for the scribes and they couldn't get enough of it. However, the Chief Planning Officer - who was still managing the bulk of the WDC relief effort - interrupted to enquire whether Fred wanted to speak to a BBC outside broadcast team camped at the entrance of the building. For Karen, the lure of a TV broadcaster trumped the power of local printed matter and she whisked him away for an interview.

Although they were disappointed about the brush off, Tom and Lena knew that they had a head start on the big story and bashed away frantically on their laptops to keep ahead of the game through their live news feeds. Both were acutely aware that this was a huge deal and that the websites of their respective publications would be in high demand.

There were also other human interest stories for the pair to explore when they roamed around the hall, and they managed to get some good quotes from the pensioners who lived in the sheltered housing development. One septuagenarian was revelling in the attention and said that it was the most exciting thing that had happened to her for at least a decade!

Various councillors from the Planning Committee were also amenable to being approached by the reporters, and Cllr Kettleborough was full of praise for everyone involved in the successful outcome,

'It's wonderful to know that we have citizens in our midst who react well when there is a hint of danger. I haven't ran this idea past the full Council yet but I am going to press for Mr Clark to receive a gallantry award. He deserves nothing less. I've also been very impressed by the response of the Emergency Services tonight, and the Council staff have worked extremely hard to set up this rest centre at very short notice.'

Shortly afterwards, the Leader of the Council, Jim Harvey, arrived at the rest centre and, after receiving a brief update from Cllr Kettleborough, he began *working the room* to acquaint himself with the temporary occupants. He also paused for a quick chat with Tom and Lena, and photo-bombed a group shot of the cadets and their parents that had been lined up by the young reporters.

Rob suspected that the wily old fox was going on the front foot to head off obvious questions about why a near tragedy had been allowed to develop in the first place. More experienced media reps would have put him on the spot straight away, and Rob assumed that Jim wouldn't have such an easy ride should an independent review of the incident be required. Regardless, he felt sorry for the Leader and he guessed that Viv Bushby would also be under the cosh when the dust settled. As public figureheads, both would probably bear the brunt of any criticism, despite the fact that Cllr Horsfield was the real villain of the piece.

While Jim was turning on the charm, Viv was driving at speed from her home to the Leisure Centre. She had left behind a household at war; her twin sons were refusing to speak to each other and insisted on using her as a reluctant go-between. The boys were continuing to lock horns over the affections of a female siren at school, and Viv cursed the deleterious effect of hormones on what had once been her affable and well adjusted offspring. In a perverse way her call to action had been a godsend because it gave her a legitimate reason to abandon her domestic peacekeeper duties, even though she was not looking forward to a confrontation with Cllr Horsfield.

While Viv was heading down the highway, the WHIP maestro cut an extremely subdued figure as he wandered the quieter areas of the Leisure Centre. He had enquired about the wellbeing of the cadets, and breathed a sigh of relief when they were all accounted for. Nevertheless, he felt guilty about dropping a major clanger and he planned to leave the building quietly as soon as the chance presented itself. Sandy saw him out of the corner of her eye and had to quell the temptation to wring his neck when he approached and asked her how she was faring. He skedaddled at pace when she turned her death ray stare on him, and sought refuge in the canteen, grabbing a hot chocolate and a Jaffa cake from a scowling Maria Milburn.

While she was catering to the masses, Maria found time to inform Charles that Viv had called ahead and wanted a quiet word with him as soon as she arrived. Not surprisingly, the blood appeared to drain from his face and he looked like he was going to faint for a moment. He retired with his drink and biscuit to a small unlit room - an ideal place for a recluse to escape from the main buzz of the hall - and he awaited his fate stoically.

When Viv finally appeared on the scene, she witnessed that everything was working like clockwork, and was content that the mind-numbing emergency resilience practice exercises at WDC had all been worthwhile. She engaged in a quick meet and greet with some of the volunteer helpers and waved to Rob, but her eyes were constantly searching for the bashful councillor who was the root cause of the whole mess. Viv eventually clocked Horsfield lurking in a darkened office adjoining the kitchen and joined him, taking care to close the door firmly and lower the blinds in the window.

Those in the know exchanged glances and surmised that Charles would be learning that Hell really did have no fury to match a woman who had been well and truly scorned. Whatever was said didn't take long but *Horseface* emerged as a shadow of the arrogant chancer who had barged into Vivs office the previous day, barking orders at all and sundry. Without glancing at anyone, he trudged wearily across the floor of the main sports hall and disappeared into the night.

Rob observed Charles's sorry departure because he had made his way towards the entrance of the Leisure Centre for a breather. He was astonished to see such a large crowd gathered in the foyer, thanks in part to the allure of social media. A BBC news reporter was talking to Fred and Karen and some people were cheering when his partner gave a thrilling account of his role in the rescue. It was a jolly affair and there was a whiff of celebration because any hint of tragedy had passed.

Rob rushed back into the building and informed Jim Harvey that the TV crew was outside, advising that it might be a good idea to provide a holding statement on air to avoid any insinuations that WDC officials were not available for comment. Jim nodded his assent, and he and Rob swiftly agreed a line to take, largely based on what Cllr Kettleborough had said to the local reporters inside the hall about the heroics of all concerned.

When the TV interviewer was offered the chance to speak with Jim, she jumped at the chance, and she was very supportive when he raised the prospect of Fred receiving some form of official recognition for his bravery. Moving on, she was about to probe suspected flaws in the Council's health and safety processes when her assistant interrupted with breaking news that the young girl in hospital would be released the following day. When she relayed the information live on air, there were loud cheers from the crowd and many pats on the back for Fred, who was busy signing autographs at the time. There was an even bigger roar of approval when the assistant passed on that the recovering patient had been given a large teddy bear by the hospital staff and she was going to name it Fred.

Rob hoped that the interview would end on that fluffy note, and got ready to usher Jim back into the building. As they were leaving, however, both men cringed when they heard the final wrap from the reporter,

'So we have a happy conclusion tonight to what could have been a very sad occasion. But, in the longer term, the public will need answers as to why officials at Woldwater District Council fell down on the job, and allowed a near fatal accident to occur. This is Anita Vernon, BBC Midshires, live from Woldchester.'

Chapter XV

Fleeting fame for Fred

The following morning, life in the WDC communications office was hectic in the extreme. The story of the rescue had been picked up by the national media, and news rooms around the country were eager to delve further into the details. Rob had risen with the lark to scan the newspapers online and was amazed at the widespread nature of the coverage - including mentions in a host of European publications and even a snippet in the Washington Post! - and he was quite amused by some of the headlines in the tabloids, his favourites being *Captain Underpants Saves the Day!* and *Right Said Fred - time to get a medal!*

He was less pleased that the Council was already being bombarded with questions about the lack of safeguards at the scene of the incident, and he convened an urgent teleconference meeting with Viv Bushby and Meera Chopra to agree the text of a defensive official statement with the aim of dampening down the criticism.

The text was posted on the Council website by 8 AM and simply read:

'Woldwater District Council is very pleased to note that all those involved in the unfortunate flooding incident at our premises last night are safe and well. We regret any inconvenience caused and we will be cooperating fully with the relevant authorities who will be investigating the incident to ensure that lessons are learned regarding our future safety precautions and interactions with the public.'

To save time handling a wave of incident-related queries, the Head of the Front of Office team arranged for Rob's statement to be incorporated into the suite of recorded messages which greeted everyone calling the Council's main telephone number. However, a lot of reporters knew the Comms Office's direct number so Rob still had a torrid time answering the phone and parroting the officially agreed text to the callers who escaped the recorded message net.

As expected, Kieran Ball of Radio Woldshire had called Rob at sparrow's fart and made his play for an interview with a Council spokesperson to supplement the blanket coverage the station was giving to the flooding incident. Mindful of the recent hatchet job that had scuppered poor old Jim Harvey, Rob coldly instructed the presenter to keep his eyes on the Council website if he required a form of words, and said he could whistle if he wanted any more help.

Kieran feigned that his feelings had been hurt and remonstrated,

'But we're local, Rob. We expect something extra given our long-standing good relations with you guys. When have we ever let you down?'

Rob took great delight in replying,

'How about every other day, Kieran? Have another listen to your interview with the WDC Leader and tell me that it isn't a car crash from his perspective. Now, you'll have to excuse me - we're really busy here and I'm sure there are other people out there who are daft enough to be crucified on air.'

To rub salt into the wound, he had a quick word on the phone with Viv Bushby and Jim Harvey and gained their consent to offer the BBC an opportunity to film a WDC Official reading the Council's official statement on the steps of the Chamber. It wasn't exactly riveting stuff but at least it would show that the Council was willing to eat humble pie in public and would also challenge sarcastic Facebook accusations that officers were sweeping the issue under the carpet.

The BBC producer selected Anita Vernon to cover the story again and - to his dismay - Rob was told to front up for the Council. Subsequently, Anita and a cameraman turned up as arranged and filmed him reading the statement in a robotic fashion. She tried to cajole Rob into providing more information without much success but didn't push things too hard because she'd heard on the grapevine that Kieran Ball had been frozen out completely. Rob's *Mogadon Special* was rather dull but it passed muster because she supplemented it successfully with some *vox pop* items featuring a couple of seniors who had been led to safety by Fred Clark.

After the stilted TV session, Rob reflected that the two local reporters from the Examiner and the Gazette hadn't bothered contacting him that day. When he considered the matter further, he wasn't totally surprised because he figured that Tom and Lena had probably managed to accumulate a large amount of exclusive insights after being at the heart of the action throughout the emergency. This suspicion was confirmed when he scanned the websites of both newspapers.

Aside from the main narratives focusing on the exploits of Fred Clark, the sites were also peppered with ancillary human interest stories and exclusive photographs which would no doubt have been hawked to the highest bidders from the national press. Rob also noticed that the Examiner had cheekily included a shot of himself and Ozzie in their photo montage, capturing them while they offered hot drinks to a group of pensioners, and he thanked God that it cast them in a reasonably good light.

In other related news on the Examiner site, *special correspondent* Tom Irwin had filed a story about the group of protesters from Little Chipping who had made their presence felt during the Planning Committee meeting. Rob thought it was highly ironic that the demonstrators would have been hogging the local headlines if the flood had not intervened. Instead, their actions had been demoted to a skimpy account which painted them as a rather heartless bunch because they had opposed the prospect of living next door to the hero of the hour, Fred Clark. The title of Tom's report perfectly summed up their ill-fated campaign - *Rabble without a cause!*

While Rob was giggling over Tom's tabloid style headline, his phone rang again and he steeled himself to fend off more unwanted flak. Instead, he was thrilled when he heard Sandy's voice on the end of the line,

'Hi Rob, it's only me. I just wondered if you were okay this morning. I expect you're a bit busy today?'

'It's bedlam, Sand, but it's good to hear from you. I'm perfectly fine - but are you alright?'

'Yes, I am - well,I think I am anyway. Look, that's not why I'm calling. I just wanted to thank you for being there for me last night. Everything that happened in the trench hit me hard when I got to the rest centre - I guess it was some kind of post traumatic shock -

but I tried hard to hold it all together until the kids were reunited with their parents. I couldn't stop feeling really guilty about everything and I was so helpless. That's when you came over and told me that everything would be okay. It was so sweet.'

'Well it was no bother honestly. I was really worried about you after what you'd been through .. and I really liked being with you anyway even though it wasn't much of a date was it? I told you before - you aren't to blame in the least, Sand. In fact, you were brilliant all night and I think you deserve a special mention in dispatches.'

'You sound like the Head at school; she dragged me into her room first thing this morning and assured me that I couldn't have done anything differently. She also said that Mr Horsfield is stepping down from the Board of Governors and everyone seems really pleased about that. But, you know, I still blame myself for not packing away earlier when the cadets were marching up and down in that bloody trench and getting bored out of their skulls.'

'It's natural to be wiser after the event, Sand. Think of all the positives that came out of the evening. I spoke to quite a few of the kids and their parents at the rest centre and they were all saying how well you did - and it's also good to know that the WDC emergency response procedures worked so smoothly when they were put to the test. Not having *Horseface* poking his nose into the school's activities will be a bonus as well.'

'I agree. That's all good stuff, but I still feel that this whole business has dented my confidence a wee bit, Rob. The Head said that I'll soon get back in the saddle and pull myself together so I hope she's right.'

'Look, you're a Glaswegian, Sand - everybody's tough as teak up there, right?'

'Och aye, allegedly. I've been away a long time, though, and you southern softies are rubbing off on me a bit.'

'There's nothing wrong with being in touch with your feelings! It's no shame to admit that you're not perfect, so you really shouldn't be too hard on yourself. It's clear to me that you need a break.'

'Ah, you must be clairvoyant! The Head told me that she would find someone else to take the Year Nines away to the Lake District on Friday because I got the rough end of the stick on the cadet drills. That means I'm free that evening if you're interested.'

'You bet! Just tell me what you want to do and whatever you fancy. I'm in.'

'Ooh, I'd prefer a surprise if I'm honest, Rob. How about calling for me at my place - you know where I live right? Number 42.'

'I'll find it. How about if I pop around at about seven o'clock?'

'That sounds fine, as long as you don't mind the Spanish inquisition from my Mum.'

'It probably wouldn't be a patch on what Viv Bushby dished out to *Horseface* at the rest centre! I'll see you on Friday then - really looking forward to it.'

Rob rang off and wandered out of the room to savour the moment. He was walking on air as he drifted down to the Front of House office to assist with updating scripts for call handlers based on his initial statement about the flooding. As he descended the stairs, he chuckled to himself when he considered the irony of his love life having been boosted by *Horseface* dropping a clanger.

Although Rob entered the FOH office in a state of mild euphoria, he was quickly brought down to Planet Earth by the frantic activity of the staff. Apart from their normal tasks, they were also deploying his defensive lines about the Council's response to the trench incident and coping with some slanderous backchat from several callers. He also noticed that they were fending off quite a few complaints about traffic congestion from neighbouring residents in the immediate vicinity of the Council headquarters.

When he queried the latter issue further, the Head of FOH said the trouble had started because a considerable number of Council parking spaces had been cordoned off temporarily to facilitate an inspection by a Health and Safety Executive official. As a result, WDC Officers arriving for work had been forced to find alternative parking for their vehicles, and many had left them in neighbouring streets.

Rob was shown a few of the postings from neighbours that were appearing on Facebook and Twitter and he soon got the drift of their reactions. One prominent message said it all: *First we have a torrent of dirty water down our street and now we have a flood of Council-owned vehicles - what the f*** is going on at Woldwater DC?*

Taking in the ramifications, Rob called Viv to bring her up to speed on the likelihood of another public relations gaffe, and she gave him the go ahead to tackle the problem swiftly on her behalf. He subsequently drafted a high priority email to all Reilly Road staff, encouraging them to leave the headquarters building immediately and work from home whenever possible. Rob also published an official apology about the vehicle congestion on the Council website, and provided a script along the same lines to assist the benighted individuals in Front of House who were getting so much grief.

Viv herself was happy to relinquish her reserved parking space at WDC because she was preparing to leave the building for a meeting at the partner council in Fordham. It pained her to hear that members of the public were venting their spleen about the administration yet again, and she feared that there would be more flak to come before things settled down again. Although Rob had briefed her on the volume of complaints, he had refrained from telling her about the extremely choice language being used on some social media postings, several of which amounted to very unpleasant personal attacks on the Chief Executive and the Leader.

Viv was confident that Rob would handle any relevant communications competently, but she was furious that Cllr Horsfield had created so much turmoil in the first place, and she was totally hacked off because ignorant commentators were laying the blame at her door. Her mood hadn't been helped by the mirthless Health and Safety Executive representative who had pitched up that morning. He had all the charm of a speak your weight machine and didn't seem to believe in the concept of human error when she tried to explain the circumstances leading up to the accident. In fact, the wretched jobsworth had already hinted that she was being viewed as the main culprit given her overall responsibility for the site. As far as Viv was concerned, the new road congestion problem created by the H&S rep's insistence on cordoning off large swathes of the car park had been the final rancid cherry on the stale cake, and she had to count to ten to stop herself screaming aloud.

However, it wasn't all bad news for Viv that morning because she had received a terse email from Charles Horsfield at the crack of dawn, informing her that he would be resigning from the Council by the end of the week. He stated that he would make a public announcement to that effect within 24 hours and asked her to refrain from sharing the news until then. Despite his request, she disclosed the advance information to Rob so that he could prepare a standard media release thanking the lummox for his service as a councillor, despite his decidedly patchy record.

On a more negative note, the resignation would pave the way for a surprise poll in South Titbury, generating additional work for the hard pressed Electoral Services team. Viv feared that a likely electoral gain for the Conservatives in Charles Horsfield's ward would give rise to an even more fragile state of affairs regarding overall control of the Council.

While she was driving to Fordham and musing on recent events, *The Shark* was also taking stock of the situation, hunkered down in the poky Reilly Road office reserved for the use of the Leader of the Opposition. He and Cllr Lesley Ashurst agreed that their tactical withdrawal from the flooded car park had proved to be the right course of action given their abortive efforts to turn the public against Fred Clark and Karen Craig. They both conceded that the Little Chipping affordable housing protest had gone to ground in light of the couple having been elevated temporarily to the status of national treasures. Despite this setback, however, Ric was focusing on future successes,

'That idiot Horsfield has messed things up for us big time. But it's grand to see that Jim and Viv are bearing the brunt of the jibes about the lack of safety precautions around the trench. I got some of our influencers at party HQ to turn up the heat on a few social media sites and that kicked things off nicely. I also heard that the locals are up in arms about the traffic congestion in the side streets this morning due to the reduction in WDC parking spaces, so that's another bonus for us.'

Lesley added gleefully,

'I bet Viv is absolutely livid at the moment. The word around the Council is that *Horseface* went behind her back and allowed the kids to access the trench without getting permission from the H&S people. Whether or not that's the truth, it suits us that she's carrying the can at the moment.'

RIc could hardly contain himself,

'Too right, Les. And it doesn't do Jim Harvey and his knuckle draggers any favours either because he agreed that Horsfield could tart up the Armed Forces Day celebrations and he just let him get on with it.'

Then he confided to her,

'Listen, Les, some of Jim's minions will be looking to drag me down into the clarts as well by inferring that I also endorsed the stupid bugger's proposal, especially since he identifies more closely with Tory policies. That's why it's important that you and the rest of our mob must refute that sort of allegation whenever you're asked.'

He continued,

'I freely admit that I didn't actually stop Charles pursuing new ways to celebrate Armed Forces Day, but that certainly doesn't mean I okayed the digging of a humongous great ditch. Between you and me, I don't think for a moment that Jim or Viv would have backed that daft idea either. I think we all assumed that old *Horseface* would make a few harmless tweaks to the ceremony and, quite frankly, it was a useful distraction to keep that pompous git off everyone's back for a while.'

'And that really worked, Ric - for once the creep wasn't hanging around my desk asking me what I was up to, staring down the front of my blouse and offering to muck in when he wasn't welcome.'

'Yeah - it was good to get him out of my hair as well in the short term. In hindsight, though, NOBODY actually took enough notice of that useless cretin's mad plan and had the sense to bawl him out. When you consider the consequences of that lack of action, the people at the top of the decision making process deserve to carry the can, - and that's why Viv and Jim are, quite rightly, in the frame to absorb the bulk of the criticism.'

Lesley nodded sagely and added,

'Let's hope we can keep it that way. You'll have to manage this whole business very carefully, Ric, and make sure all of our members stick rigidly to your version of events just in case anyone comes sniffing around. I'll spread the word about your lack of direct involvement in this farce and hope that it sticks.'

Ric agreed,

'I think I should call them all in and brief them as soon as I can. I'm sure they'll be quite receptive because it's a major gain for us when the Leader and the Chief Exec are being made to look pretty incompetent at the moment. We've got them both on the back foot in the eyes of the electorate, and we have to try and kick them some more while they're down.'

'How do you mean to do that, Ric?'

'Well, we can keep the social media pot boiling a little longer on the trench saga and I've got another tasty trick up my sleeve, Les. I think I can really upset the apple cart good and proper, but I just need to do a bit more research before I'm ready to roll.'

Chapter XVI

Poll preparations proliferate

As anticipated, Cllr Horsfield's resignation from WDC caused a stir when it was announced formally the next day. He had succeeded in keeping the announcement under wraps so it was something of a surprise to fellow councillors in both the Coalition and Tory ranks when it was announced. Having been informed in advance about his decision, Viv had promised Charles that she would sit on it until he was ready to share the revelation with the world at large. With this in mind, she had sworn Rob to secrecy when she tipped him off in advance on the basis that he would be fully prepared to deal with any fallout.

When *Horseface* finally went public with his decision, Rob was well briefed to handle queries from the news media, and he was astonished by the amount of attention being focused on the disclosure. In normal circumstances, a ward member standing down would be small potatoes in the eyes of the general public. On this occasion, Cllr Horsfield's demise triggered a bow wave of coverage across the county and beyond. There was even a flurry of interest in his stepping down as a school governor.

Initially, the main media angle continued to be the near fatal accident that had precipitated Charles's exit. On a secondary level, however, relinquishing his Council seat generated considerable speculation about the implications for WDC, especially because it could alter the overall make-up of the administration. The public was reminded that a gain for Cllr Sharkey's Conservatives would give them 16 seats, making them the joint largest party. The Lib Dems would still be able to cling to power by virtue of their own 16 seats and their two Labour Party supporters but it would mean that Jim Harvey's hand on the tiller would become increasingly unsteady.

Ric Sharkey could hardly believe his luck. He was managing to steer clear of any allegations linking him to the Armed Forces Day mess, and he had now been presented with a great opportunity to strengthen his party's standing at Reilly Road. He called his partner Nadine and told her excitedly about the unexpected windfall. As he anticipated, she whooped with joy before reverting seamlessly to her default Machiavellian mode, providing him with expert advice on the best way forward in the run up to the by-election,

'Get your arse down to the Party HQ, sweetie, and seek out the most effective grassroots activists - that dishy Wayne Kerr will be able to help on that ...and, oh my gosh, he's probably the best candidate for the South Titbury ward as well when I come to think of it! You, Wayne and the others should form the core of an election task group and I'll help you out with the comms and strategy stuff - and the Titbury-based local yokels at HQ will also be able to get some feedback on the highest priority issues in their area. Lesley's your best bet to help spearhead the campaign at the strategic level and make sure that moron Cllr Harrison keeps his gob shut. Now, as far as the timing is concerned....'

'My God - slow down for a minute, Nadine. I can't keep up! I think that's a fantastic idea about Wayne, though. He lives in South Titbury and a candidate from their own backyard always goes down well with the voters.'

'Excellent - I had a feeling that he was a local so we've got a head start. Mind you, because *Horseface* won a majority there I'm guessing that there must be a big following for quasi-fascists in that shithole. We'll have to toughen up our messages to chime a bit more with the WHIP political philosophy but I'm sure that Wayne can carry that off. Now, what about the opposition?'

'No idea yet, darling. It's early days. Charles won handsomely last time around but he was a one-off. The other WHIP fanatics are mostly young crackheads from what I can gather so we're certainly not aware of Horsfield Version 2.0 waiting in the wings. Given a fair wind there won't be an independent with any real clout running, and we should be able to see off the Lib Dems and Labour. I'm totally convinced that we can fill the void left by Charles and nab the seat by a comfortable margin, provided we box clever of course. I can't wait, my love - this is going to be epic!'

Elsewhere in the building, Cllr Jim Harvey was conducting a conversation about the forthcoming by-election with his Lib Dem Deputy Leader and Planning Committee Chair, Cllr Don Hilley, and the Council Chair, Cllr Keith Wharton. The tone of their debate was much less lively, and Jim was especially subdued,

'Gentlemen, I think we're shafted here. Horsfield may have been a bit of a clown but he won by a comfortable majority last time out, and the ward was always a Tory stronghold before he came along. Unless another WHIP camp follower upsets the apple cart, Sharkey's guys will be a shoo in if they get their act together. The sly sod is dining out on all this flood emergency hype at the moment, and….'

Cllr Hilley interjected,

'Ric's like effing Teflon. He was better placed than you and Viv to prevent Charles's crazy stunt and I daresay he could have knocked the whole thing on the head before it went tits up - and for some reason we're the ones getting it in the neck in the papers. We need to find a way to skewer that sneaky git or we've lost that ward election before we even start.'

Jim raised his eyebrows and confessed,

'Well, that's a lot easier said than done. Ric's a sharp cookie and he'll be pulling out all the stops to secure that seat for the Tories. We'll have to get our thinking caps on to see if we can knacker them somehow.'

Socialist Cllr Keith Wharton chipped in with a useful preliminary step,

117

'Look, for starters I'll make sure that my party doesn't put up a candidate. That means the moderate vote won't be split between Labour and the Lib Dems so you've got something to work with. I don't think that will be enough to tip the balance by a long chalk, but at least you don't have our guys to worry about.'

Having said his piece, Cllr Wharton made his exit from the room. He was still recovering from a nasty bout of Covid that he'd picked up on a goodwill visit to a nursing home, and the last thing he wanted was the hassle of fielding a Labour candidate while he was recuperating, especially in a ward where his party had bombed for decades. Keith was therefore content to leave the fool's errand to the Lib Dems, and his biggest priority of the day was whether to opt for a cup of breakfast tea or Earl Grey when he tucked into a slice of his wife's delicious carrot cake on his return to the family home.

Jim and Don suspected that the Chair had an ulterior motive when he made his grand gesture, but they were, nevertheless, grateful for his withdrawal in the knowledge that he would lay himself open to heavy criticism from some of Labour's ultra left brigade in Titbury. Both men thanked their stars that they had such a good working relationship with a Coalition partner who could always be relied upon to take a pragmatic stance.

The two men agreed to meet again soon at a brainstorming session to devise possible lines of attack for the by-election, in the knowledge that the cupboard was looking incredibly bare when it came to ideas for countering the bias towards right wing politics in South Titbury. Worse still was the fact that they were nearing completion of their plans for a WDC redundancy programme which would result in further cuts to several services and that would probably not go down too well with the public at large.

Down in the Democratic Services office, the officer in charge, Nora Allen, was briefing her small team on the forthcoming shindig in South Titbury. She was confident that they could cope with the extra burden of the by-election, even though they were knee deep in a slew of mandatory tasks related to the updating of the electoral register in the district.

Nora was a natural delegator and prided herself on having such an efficient team to carry out the chores that formed the daily grind in her office. She empowered her deputy Sally and her colleague Katrin to deal with most of those tasks, while she was able to devote most of her time to keeping the peace between the Coalition and the Tories - a job that had become increasingly challenging since the coming of Ric Sharkey. Because of *The Shark's* antics in particular, her phone always seemed to be off the hook as councillors from both sides of the political divide bent her ear about the failings of their counterparts. As a result, she knew most of the hefty WDC Code of Conduct by heart, having had to thumb through so much of it to resolve a host of petty disputes.

Nora regularly dragged poor Meera Chopra into many of the ridiculous spats between the Coalition ward members and the Conservatives, seeking both her legal input and a helping hand to calm the waters on procedural disputes. She and Nora were sick to the back teeth of the political posturing and one-upmanship that now typified life at Reilly Road, and they often complained that it was getting in the way of them being able to do any sort of constructive work themselves.

Despite her daily trials and tribulations, the Legal Advisor was in a good frame of mind when she spoke with Nora about the forthcoming by-election. Meera greeted the news of Cllr Horsfield's sudden resignation as a chink of unexpectedly bright light in a very grey world, and prayed that a much less obnoxious candidate would succeed the WHIP demagogue. Nora agreed that *Horseface's* departure would be a blessing for many officers who had crossed his miserable path.

However, Meera's erstwhile cheery mood darkened somewhat when she returned to her office and was informed that Horsfield was waiting outside and wanted to meet her before he left the building that day. Ever the professional, she steeled herself to confront her nemesis and hoped that the meeting would be short and sweet. When he entered the room, he tried to lull her into a false sense of security as he opened the discussion in a low key fashion with a string of courteous platitudes. She wasn't fooled for a minute and was anticipating a swift downturn in the quality of the conversation. A few alarm bells rang for her as soon as Horsfield decided to close the door without her permission, and he immediately dropped his nice guy routine,

'I expect you're wondering why I want to speak with you, sweetheart, so here goes... before I leave this building today I just want to make sure that you know where you stand from now on. You think I can't mess things up for you any more, but you're mistaken, petal. There's more than one way to crack a nut and you can be sure that you haven't seen the last of me.'

Meera was baffled,

'I don't know why you are so hostile towards me. What have I done to upset you so much?'

Horsfield replied in an admonitory tone,

'Just the fact that you're holding down a senior job that a proper British person can do perfectly well is enough to upset any true patriot. You lot were just about bearable years ago when we were short of grafters to operate the buses, sweep the streets, and run grotty little corner shops … but you're all getting above yourselves too much these days. We didn't vote to regain our sovereignty in 2016 and then allow the likes of you to run the blasted country. I ask you - an Asian soddin' Prime Minister! Who saw that coming? We want our country back, sugar - and the sooner you folks take that hint the better.'

Meera kept her cool and responded in measured tones,

'You may not have noticed, Cllr Horsfield, but many of the Asian communities in places like Bradford and Birmingham also voted to leave the EU. Some did it because a plonker told them fairy tales about extra funding for the NHS and posted his baseless claims on the side of a whackin' great battle bus. But a lot of people from the Indian sub-continent signed up for Brexit because they saw it as an opportunity to strengthen ties between the UK and other Commonwealth nations. Whether you like it or not, the UK can't survive without outside help and we're not looking too clever now that a lot of European workers have upped sticks and gone back home. Many second and third generation Brits feel that this is their chance to take up that slack and also do well for themselves.'

Horsfield harrumphed and raised his voice,

'Well not on your terms, Missy. Listen carefully - I want to play my small part in stopping the rot and that's where you come in. You and your family are denying real British people the opportunity to gain control of our country again and I can't stand back and let that happen. You should all watch your backs from now on. I'll be on your case until you all clear off back to your filthy disease-ridden shanty towns in India.'

Meera was incensed when he made his threat and shouted,

'Get out of my office now, you crazy moron! I hope that our paths never cross again - and if they do and you cause any harm to me or any of my relatives, I'll use all my legal nous to make sure that you are punished.'

He smirked and walked out of the room, slamming the door behind him. After his dramatic exit, Meera sat silently for a while and sobbed gently, wondering if he really meant what he had said.

Chapter XVII

Love is in the hair

Friday night rolled around at long last and Rob could hardly contain his excitement as he dressed for an evening out with Sandy at arguably the best - and certainly the most expensive - eatery in town. Despite his mother's insistence that he should wear a suit and tie, he opted for a more casual look on the advice of his former wife Maria. She was keeping her fingers crossed that Rob might have found a life partner at long last and had taken her ex under her wing to smarten him up for the special occasion. Looking in the mirror before he left the house, Rob was reasonably pleased with his appearance, especially a more flattering hairstyle that didn't emphasise his widow's peak so much. He told himself that things were on the up in the romance stakes, and he wasn't going to blow it this time.

He arrived at the bungalow occupied by Sandy and her mother right on time and rang the doorbell tentatively. A few seconds later, an older version of his date welcomed him into the house and, as predicted by Sandy, began firing questions at him in a strong Scottish brogue,

'Sandra hasnae told me much aboot ye, hen, and I was just wonderin' whether yer a good Catholic boy or a Proddie?'

'Er, neither actually Mrs Staveley. I'm not really into organised religion.'

'Weel, at least yer no' a miserable Proddie son. And tell me, dae ye have yer ain teeth?'

'Ah, yes. Last time I looked in the mirror. Yes, they're all mine I think.'

'And what does yer Pa do for a livin'?'

'My Dad? Oh, he died a few years ago. It's just me and Mum now.'

At that point, Sandy burst into the room and upbraided her mother for giving Rob such a hard time,

'For goodness sake, Ma. You're doing your usual twenty questions. How many times do I have to tell you?'

'I'm only lookin' after yer interests, ma wee lamb. Anyway, he seems like a braw lad and you're right aboot his nice eyes.'

When this private confession came to light, Sandy looked embarrassed and Rob smiled at her to show that he sympathised with her dilemma.

They departed hastily but were still within range of Ma Staveley's parting shot,

'I saw yer on the TV the other day, son, when thon wee lass nearly drooned ye ken, and ye read oot a statement. I told Sandra that ye weren't too shabby fer a gobshite but yer should stop pretendin' that you've got a broom shoved up yer arse.'

Sandy confided later that he had been paid a great compliment and they laughed about his interrogation as they drove to the restaurant. She had been expecting the Chinese that Rob had recommended a few days earlier and was thrilled when they arrived at Le Bistro, the most exclusive joint in Woldchester.

After the waiter escorted them to their table, Sandy took in the lavish decor and complimented Rob on his choice of venue. She had clearly regained her bounce after her recent ordeal and was looking forward to her posh nosh experience. They indulged in some small talk while perusing the menus and were very comfortable in each other's company. Sandy told Rob that his new haircut took years off him and he admired her new dress. All things considered, the evening was going much better than he could ever have imagined until he caught sight of someone who might spoil the whole show.

Sandy detected the change in his expression at once and asked,

'What's up Rob? You look like you've seen an evil spirit or something.'

'Not quite - but almost. It's Cllr RIc Sharkey. He's over in the corner with a woman and I think he's trying to catch my eye. Damn... he's waving at me now. I think he's coming over.'

'What's so bad about him? He looks harmless enough.'

'Wait and see, Sand. You'll soon know why he's called *The Shark*. You just watch him, he'll be trying to pump me for any inside information he can get about the aftermath of the flood, and his techniques will make your Ma look like a rank bad amateur... and he's walking across to our table now!

As anticipated, Cllr Sharkey had crossed the floor to fraternise with the young couple,

'Ah, Rob. How nice to see you here ... and your young lady too. I caught your stellar appearance on telly the other day. Bad old business this trench thing isn't it? Your poor boss must be a bit put out eh?'

Rob was trying to give nothing away,

'I'm confident that she'll get over it, Cllr Sharkey. She's used to dealing with tricky situations, as you well know.'

'Yes, you're right of course. I'm sure she's got a lot on her plate at the moment but she always seems to muddle through somehow. I heard that she even found time to host a staff development presentation the other day. How did that go then?'

'Oh, I was indisposed so I didn't get to see much of it.'

'What a shame. I would have liked to hear your honest opinion. You see, I just have a feeling that hiring Roger Whatshisname to improve performance isn't the right route to follow. We're much better off with more scientific methods if we want to become a more agile workforce. In fact, I was just talking the other day to a chap called Joe Baxter and he says that he can increase WDC's efficiency by 40% through the use of a new technological breakthrough that monitors officer output. Have you come across him at all?'

'Yes I've met him. He popped into the office the other day and had a word with Cllr Harvey about his scheme. I was called in to discuss the comms angle.'

'How interesting. Joe's a revelation isn't he? What did Jim Harvey reckon?'

'That's not really my business, Cllr Sharkey. I was only summoned to talk about my specialist field and Mr Baxter seemed to be doing most of the talking anyway. I did pick up that Cllr Harvey would be meeting the Chief Exec to discuss Joe's offer when she has a bit of spare time, and I daresay you'll be in the loop at some stage because you made the recommendation. So I expect Mr Baxter will know the outcome in the fullness of time.'

'Ah, that's splendid. Always happy to help you know. Much better than hiring some charlatan motivator who just wants to line his pockets. Well, I'll let you get on then. I need to nip back to see what Nadine wants to order. By the way, I would recommend the Chateaubriand for two - it's fantastic. Goodnight both. Take care.'

Once he appeared to be out of earshot, Sandy pulled a face and whispered,

'God, I see what you mean about him. He gives me the creeps! His partner looks stunning but I think she could be a right madam too. She was staring at us like she had a bad smell under her nose.'

'Yes she's a bit up herself by the looks. Do you know, I'm sure I've seen her somewhere before but I can't recall where. Probably a Council function or something like that.'

'They're both a wee bit sinister aren't they?'

'Just like Joe Baxter's business improvement methods that he keeps on about – straight out of Orwell's 1984. *The Shark* wants to lumber the Council with disgustingly inhumane plans for cutting corners that might do a lot of damage to the quality of our services, and there'll be savage reductions in the staff headcount. But nobody in the media cares a jot about those issues, even though we seem to be big news at the moment.'

The intervention by Ric had killed the mood slightly but Rob was relieved when the momentum picked up again quickly as they ordered their meals and he pointedly ignored the Chateaubriand on the menu. The wine loosened their tongues and they both confessed that the flooding incident hadn't been entirely bad because it had brought them together on a very enjoyable date.

When the evening came to a close and Rob walked Sandy to her door, she gave him a long lingering kiss and told him to call her soon. Rob could see a light burning in the hall and didn't hang around to face his third inquisition of the evening. Nevertheless, he was a really happy bunny because Sandy had agreed to go and see a movie with him. Just before she closed her front door, however, he had a sudden brainwave and suggested that they could go one better and attend the WDC Chairman's swanky charity ball instead. For good measure, he added that he could bag two complimentary tickets if she was interested.

Sandy's eyes lit up at the prospect of a special evening out in a posh frock and she was thrilled to bits. If he had been truthful, Rob would have disclosed that glitzy events weren't really his sort of thing, but he 'd anticipated that it would be right up Sandy's street. What he didn't tell her was that he would only be attending because Cllr Wharton had asked him to take the official photographs (another job he had taken on at Reilly Road because of staffing cutbacks) and he prayed that he could wangle another free ticket somehow, after bragging that it was all sorted.

Chapter XVIII

Having a ball

There was excitement in the air as the clock ticked down to the charity ball. The WDC Chair, Cllr Wharton, was fussing and fretting a lot more than usual in the run up to the event, but he was extremely pleased that all the tickets had been sold, thanks in part to the sterling work done by the Council Comms team in generating sufficient publicity. When Rob asked him about the prospect of obtaining an extra ticket he revealed that Cllr Horsfield had recently returned his invite and that Sandy could take it up free of charge because the fee paid by the disgraced Councillor was non-refundable. He insisted that Rob should still get there early to take photos of guests arriving and his *plus one* for the evening would have to fend for herself for a short while.

GIven that stipulation, Rob told Sandy that she had to be ready to depart a good hour before the ball's official start time. He was quite sheepish when he explained why they had to make such an early entrance, but she was more than happy to do her own thing for a while, and said that she was well versed in making small talk with people she didn't know at school functions.

When he called for her at the Staveley bungalow early in the evening, Sandy's mother greeted him at the door and invited him in for a few minutes because his date was just finishing her pre-ball preparations. She noticed that Rob had hired a rather smart dinner jacket for the evening and remarked that he really looked the part. To his relief, she wasn't deploying her previously irksome waterboarding tactics, and they passed the time easily, touching on a range of anodyne topics, including the recent spell of bad weather and the rising price of a portion of fish and chips.

The air of mundanity was dispelled when Sandy walked into the room and Rob paused in mid sentence,

'Haddock is normally more expensive but I like cod better...wow, oh, my word!'

129

Sandy had never looked so adorable. She had pinned up her auburn hair to reveal an elegant neckline, and her make up looked superb, courtesy of the Frenchwoman on the cosmetic counter of the department store in Woldchester. Best of all was her dress - a black figure-hugging number that she had borrowed from a friend who wasn't short of a bob or two. The outfit was enhanced through the addition of a pair of Jimmy Choo shoes that she had tracked down in a charity store. She knew that she would never be able to compete with Cllr Sharkey's dinner companion in the glamour stakes, but she was very satisfied with her end result and relished the effect she was having on Rob and her mother. Mrs Staveley was the first to comment on her appearance,

'Yer look absolutely incredible, ma wee pet. Like someone oot of one of thae magazines about the lifestyles of rich folk.'

Rob agreed enthusiastically ,

'What a stunner you are, Sandy! And you look so different with your hair done like that. You know, you deserve a much better escort than me when you dress as well as that.'

Mrs Staveley nodded vigorously in agreement, but Sandy leapt to Rob's defence,

'Hey, Robster, don't beat yourself up so much. You're pretty damn good yourself when you scrub up a bit and put on some decent clobber. Anyway, we'd better get going if you want to be there on schedule to take all of those photos that the Council Chairman wants.'

They arrived at the venue - the Woldchester Assembly Rooms - in time for Rob to have a quick word with Cllr Wharton, about the best angles for shots of the revellers making their grand entrance. Sandy was the first guest to be captured on the WDC official camera and then she left Rob to mingle on her own while he began to click away when other invitees started to arrive. On each occasion, Keith Wharton was on hand to do a *grip and grin* pose with the guests, and it took about forty minutes to complete the task. By that time, Rob noticed that a number of younger male attendees were circling around Sandy like flies around a honey pot and he was pleased when she looked up, excused herself and rushed over to him.

'This is all good fun so far, Rob. I've been propositioned three times but I said that I was waiting for my boyfriend and it seemed to do the trick.'

'And is that true - is that what you think I am?'

'Of course, silly. I wouldn't have come here with you otherwise. Come on, let's have some fun now that you're done with your chores. We can grab a canape and a drink before the meal if you hurry.'

They managed to chase down a glass of white after a morsel or two and indulged in idle chatter with a few of the guests, including one or two lecherous councillors who were eyeing up Sandy for a dance later on.

As expected, the person who really turned heads was Nadine Hurley. She wore a gold sequined dress that sparkled in the light and wouldn't have looked out of place on the catwalk of a London Fashion Week show. When Rob had taken her photograph on arrival, he noticed that she had a distinct way of posing for the camera, taking care to stretch her neck to avoid any sort of skin folds showing. In comparison, Cllr Sharkey looked like her valet, but he didn't seem to mind as he was lapping up the admiring glances that were directed towards the couple.

Not for the first time, Rob wondered why Nadine's face was familiar from a previous occasion but he didn't want to wrack his brains too much when he was trying to focus his attention on his newly-anointed girlfriend, who was clutching his arm.

The guests finally sat down for a remarkably tasty three course meal, and the wine and conversation flowed freely. Cllr Wharton was at the head of the top table and made a short speech thanking everyone for supporting the charity ball; he provided pithy descriptions of the two good causes that would benefit from the event, and also informed the guests that there would be a charity auction after the meal.

When the plates were finally cleared, the auction got underway and enough guests were sufficiently merry to bid generous sums of money for the lots on offer. Perhaps the standout item was a carved wooden bench dating from Victorian times, allegedly owned by the late Alice Shearer, one of Woldshire's most famous former residents. Nadine fell in love with the bench at first sight and she whispered to *The Shark* that it would look marvellous in the lobby of their new lakeside home.

Prompted by his partner, Ric started the bidding at £200 and Cllr Jim Harvey upped the offer straight away to £250. This caused Sharkey to raise the stakes again and Harvey followed suit. It soon became evident that a mini bidding war was developing between the Tory supremo on one side and the Lib Dem chief on the other, and there were gasps of amazement when the price of the lot soared past the £1,000 mark and was still rising.

Nadine was beginning to look less serene after the bidding reached £1,500 and signalled to Ric that they had reached their ceiling. Despite his partner's reluctance to continue, *The Shark* was loath to throw in the towel and he punched the air when he finally secured his prize for £2,350. As the hammer came down, he glanced triumphantly at Jim Harvey and was extremely disappointed to see that his rival didn't seem to care much at all. In fact, some of Jim's colleagues were shaking him by the hand and congratulating him on the part he had played in raising so much money for the Chairman's charities.

Ric was furious that they were so elated and, when the auction concluded, he stormed across to the Lib Dem posse and vented his anger,

'You must be very proud of yourself Harvey! You forced up the price of that bloody tat on purpose because you noticed that Nadine fancied it.'

Jim didn't appreciate being interrupted so rudely at a social event, and replied curtly,

'Put it behind you, Sharkey. It's for charity, man, so think of the good you've done.'

Jim turned away which had the effect of infuriating Ric even more, and he bawled out,

'Yeah. I can appreciate the charitable angle, but there was no need to hang me out to dry, you bastard.'

The Leader took a deep breath and tried not to get involved in a public spat. He then responded patiently,

'Listen,Cllr Sharkey, it was an auction so I was perfectly entitled to make an offer for anything I wanted. If you didn't notice, I shelled out £650 for a painting that is probably only worth about £50. It's for charity for heaven's sake - just grow a pair and get over it.'

Ric felt his hackles rise and was tempted to throw a punch at Jim, but he reined himself in and returned to his table after he caught a glimpse of Nadine beckoning to him frantically. She had a face like thunder and was obviously not pleased with his petulant display in front of so many influential people. Within minutes, the couple had excused themselves as soon as they had concluded the purchase of the bench and made the delivery arrangements. Before departing, Ric couldn't resist one last swipe at Jim when he was passing near his table,

'You might think that what you did was very clever, Harvey. But you won't be smiling when your guy gets a good hammerin in the South Titbury by-election. I may have lost that silly little battle tonight but I'm going to win the whole damn war - just you wait and see.'

Rob and Sandy watched the whole infantile scenario unfold and then they laughed like drains when Cllr Sharkey and his partner disappeared into the night. Cllr Wharton didn't stay much longer either because he had overdone things slightly in the run up to the big night and was feeling the effects of so much hard work. His last act of the evening was to announce the start of the dancing and -

right on cue - *Rockin' All Over the Wold* bounced onto the stage to perform a live set, with Ozzie performing lead vocals and his mate Gibbo assigned to bass guitar.

Guests who knew the pair prepared for the worst, but they experienced an unexpected surprise as the band struck up *Let Me Entertain You* and churned out a very passable version of the Robbie Williams original. Rob could hardly credit that the two layabouts he mixed with in the pub were capable of such a fine standard of musicianship, and he and Sandy joined the throng of merrymakers on the dance floor. Each song that the band played was welcomed with a roar of recognition from the highly appreciative crowd, and the performers were cheered to the rafters.

Just before the end of the set, Ozzie revealed his impish nature by dedicating the final song to t*he young lovers Rob and Sandy who are embarking on a new romance tonight.* Rob was mortified and could feel his red face radiating like a beacon, but he was relieved when he twigged that Sandy enjoyed the special mention,and she was ecstatic when the band played *Islands in the Stream* - one of her all-time favourite songs.

Looking into Rob's eyes, while holding him close on the dance floor, she kissed him on the lips and said,

'Well, Robster Lobster. We've got our very own song now. I guess that means we really are a bit of an item.'

Chapter XIX

Purdah pain

135

After the excitement of the ball, Monday morning rolled around all too soon and the weekly grind got underway at Reilly Road once again. For Rob, there was a lot less work to tackle than usual. Since the announcement of the by-election in South Titbury, his task list had eased considerably because the Council was entering a period known as *Purdah*. This meant that the Communications Office had to refrain from issuing any information that could be construed as publicity which might seek to influence voters. The embargo placed a temporary hold on the *Keep Woldwater Tidy* initiative - masterminded by Cllr McGrath - which the Council had been ready to launch, and a much anticipated announcement from the Leader about the provision of more social housing in the north of the District was also put on ice.

Rob was still able to answer external queries of a factual nature but he had to make absolutely sure that he didn't provide responses that would in any way identify favourably or unfavourably with candidates or parties. To ensure that the service remained squeaky clean, he advised Ozzie to forward all external queries to him and then Rob made sure that he consulted fully with the Legal Advisor and the Head of Democratic Services on any potentially tricky issues.

Most of his media contacts were familiar with the *Purdah* restrictions and tended not to bother Rob as much as usual because he was shackled by red tape. This left him with more time to explore other aspects of his work, but he also found himself at a bit of a loose end. Posters on notice boards around the building reminded staff that Roger Pitt was returning later that day for two follow-up *Future Journey* presentations, and a good number of officers were preparing to attend. This time around, Rob had no excuses for ducking out, so he made arrangements to spend some time at the first session scheduled for lunch time.

Although Ozzie was normally very lukewarm about any sort of corporate gathering, he was like a cat on hot bricks prior to Roger Pitt's next appearance, and he was looking forward to seeing the maestro strut his stuff again at the afternoon session. Rob had never been able to motivate his junior in similar fashion so he was quite curious to witness Roger's *wow factor* in the flesh. He trotted across to the Chamber in receptive mode and took a seat next to the Democratic Services Head, Nora Allen, who was looking a tad less impressed than many of the attendees,

'What a waste of time, Rob. We've got loads of extra work on with the by-election coming up and we've been strong-armed into coming here by Viv. I honestly can't see the point.'

Rob didn't agree as wholeheartedly as she expected,

'I have my doubts as well, Nora, but I'm keeping an open mind until I've seen this guy in action. Young Ozzie is a Damascene convert even though it's debatable whether he's picking up any of the learning points. He harps on about Roger Pitt's entertainment value all the time so I don't think it will be dull anyway.'

They stopped talking at that point because Viv Bushby had appeared with Roger and, after she introduced him to the staff, the presentation began.

Roger waited for silence to descend, and then paused for a couple of seconds for dramatic effect before addressing his audience,

'There's this oil millionaire in Texas and he never does anything by halves. His son has a fifth birthday coming up and he tells his Dad that he wants a pedal car. But his old man wants to impress the lad so he goes out and buys him the Ford motor company! The next year his kid is coming up to six and wants a baseball bat, but the father wants to make a grander gesture again and buys him the New York Yankees franchise. By now the kid is getting older and wiser and he insists that all he wants for his seventh birthday is a cowboy outfit with absolutely no frills, so his father lowers his sights at long last and purchases Woldwater District Council.'

The punchline was greeted with a ripple of laughter from some quarters and a gasp of incredulity from others. Roger waited for the reaction to die down and then went on the offensive,

'Do you really want people to think in that way about WDC? I've seen enough of your organisation to know that it's full of dedicated professionals who strive against the odds to make a difference to people's lives. And yet, if you fail to grasp the opportunities presented by working in tandem with your opposite numbers in West Fordham, then the only way is down. And, yes, that means being perceived as a load of shoddy cowpokes. By the way, on the same subject, did you hear about the paper cowboy? He got done for rustling!'

Polite giggling followed his throwaway gag and Rob could see why Roger succeeded as a motivational speaker. He had a good line of patter and managed to touch on tricky subjects without boring the pants off people. The presentation continued in the same vein and, despite his natural inclination towards cynicism, Rob was impressed by what he heard.

Towards the end of the session, Roger invited Nora's two colleagues from Democratic Services to come forward and gave them each a large gold-coloured ring. He then turned to the audience and said,

'My glamorous assistants, Sally and Katrin, are going to show you what joint working is all about. You will see that they are each holding a large ring. Now they are going to toss them into the air simultaneously and let's see what happens.'

At his command, the two women threw their rings into the air and, as they were descending, Roger caught them with one hand and then displayed to everyone that they had become linked together. Sally and Katrin both looked rather surprised and other onlookers were mystified as to how he had managed the sleight of hand. He held the conjoined rings aloft and said triumphantly,

'Let's imagine that one of those rings is Woldwater Council and the other is West Fordham. You saw with your own eyes that they can exist separately, but when they were up in the air they could have easily fallen to the floor and broken apart. I'm here to make sure that doesn't happen - my aim - with your help - is to catch them both when they are in a state of change and bring them together so that they are stronger and more resilient. Ladies and gentlemen, I'm Roger Pitt and I hope I've demonstrated to you the value of joint working.'

The audience applauded when he concluded the presentation, and Rob and Nora clapped along with the rest, even though both agreed that the final flourish may have been slightly over the top. As he glanced around him, Rob swore he caught sight of the Lib Dem spear-carrier, Cllr Lesley Ashurst. peeking through the glass door of the Chamber and he wondered if she had witnessed the grand finale.

He returned to his desk and was bombarded with queries from Ozzie about the event. Rob didn't want to spoil any of the gags lined up, and told his young assistant that he would enjoy the show but advised him to pay more attention to the references about the overall aims of the development programme. This included the requirement to begin the personalised training module that Ozzie had been avoiding for days.

Rob could tell that Ozzie had been quite idle during his absence and it didn't look like he had scanned the media that morning to check on any references to WDC or other matters with a bearing on their work. This became apparent when the phone rang and Lena Montgomery came on the line chasing up a story about a local protestor, which she had published in the online edition of the Gazette earlier that morning,

'I expect you've seen my article about this anonymous chap who goes around various locations in the area, highlighting the reduction in public toilet facilities?'

'Er, no. Lena. We're just catching up with various news items and that one has pissed, er I mean passed us by.'

'Well, apparently he tracks down abandoned toilet blocks, relieves himself against the walls, and then he gets out an aerosol spray and leaves a message that states *The Phantom Urinator Says NO to toilet closures.* We've got photos of his handiwork from residents in several villlages.'

'Well, thanks for telling me. I'll make sure that I talk to the relevant Head of Service to get the graffiti removed as soon as possible.'

'That's good to know, Rob. But that's not why I'm calling. You see, this phantom guy has asked the Gazette to support his campaign for the reopening of all the public conveniences in the district that were closed to save money. He claims that your Council is doing untold damage to mental health.'

'Now hang on a minute...has this so-called mystery man got anything to do with efforts to stir things up on the South Titbury by-election campaign trail?'

'Hey Rob, you should know that I can't disclose my sources ..but he does claim that he's an independent crusader with no ties to any political party, and he says that he's making a stand against an *uncaring and morally bankrupt authority staffed by idiots.* You know, I think he's got a point when you consider the mental health issues that he's bringing to light. Apparently, there are local residents who are now too scared to venture out to the shops because they might need to spend a penny and there's hardly anywhere to go.'

Lena knew that she was in the ascendancy and added,

'There's only one public convenience left in Titbury and two in Woldchester, and there's every chance that they could be vandalised and out of action. And, on top of everything, it now costs 20p to use the toilets when they used to be free. We need a quote from your Lords and Masters please. I'm running a follow-up this afternoon.'

Rob huffily told Lena that he wasn't really in a position to respond during *Purdah* but she countered that it might be appropriate in this instance because she was offering WDC an opportunity to *counteract misleading, controversial or extreme information.* She had obviously been reading the official guidance and figured that her story qualified on the *controversial* count at least. Rob conceded the point reluctantly and told Lena that he would try to chase up a factual response for her.

His next port of call was the office of Albert Suddick, the officer who was Head of Service for The Environment and Communities. Albert had just received an early heads up about the latest national fly tipping statistics, broken down by local authority areas, and Woldwater appeared to be in danger of slipping down towards the bottom of the pile. He was concerned about the external reaction when the figures came to light and was working on a mitigation report for Viv Bushby.

When he heard that Rob wanted to see him about a hostile media query, Albert naturally assumed that there had been a leak about the illegal dumping of waste and launched into a fierce diatribe,

'It's not bloody fair, Rob. We're in a rural district and we have to manage one of the largest areas covered by any local authority in the whole bleedin' country. That's 420 square miles for our Environment Wardens to get around and there's only a few of them left these days to keep on top of it all. We can't be everywhere and it only takes a few numpties to....'

'Woah, Albert. Whatever you're moaning about doesn't sound great, but I'm here to enquire about our public toilets.'

142

'Oh, ask away, Rob. Anything but soddin' fly tipping is okay with me today. I've already had *The Shark* in here raving about a zero tolerance policy for offenders as if he's just invented the concept. I'm more than happy to deal with questions about the odd WC here and there.'

'I don't think you'll be saying that when you find out the specifics of the query.'

Albert listened to the precis of Rob's conversation with Lena and didn't look too impressed after Rob had finished - in fact, he almost threw a hissy fit,

'Give me strength, for God's sake. Who raked up this old chestnut and dressed it in new clothes? Mental health risks eh? I thought the closures were all done and dusted after we announced the cutbacks last year ... and we really got it in the neck at the time if you recall.'

Rob agreed that the Council had endured an extremely rough ride when it introduced a package of savings that decimated many aspects of its service provision. Jim Harvey had reluctantly wielded the axe following years of reductions in funding from central government, together with severe restrictions on permitted increases to the Council Tax bands. Casualties included a thriving leisure centre in Titbury, a network of Memory Clubs for people with dementia, Dog and other Environmental Wardens, the Pest Control service, Tourism Office staff, and public lavatories.

Albert was still on the warpath, and continued his rant,

'Let me tell you something, Rob, in words of one syllable - WE HAD NO CHOICE! It costs a king's bloody ransom to provide public toilets, even when we charge people a fee for using them. Do you know how much it costs to maintain just three toilet blocks per year, including maintenance, staffing and other overheads?'

'No idea, Albert. Maybe £20,000?'

'Try multiplying that by seven and you might get close to the figure. And don't tell me that we must be getting a good bit of that money back on account of all the 20p pieces that people shell out to use our loos - that brings in about £40,000 so we're down on the deal by about £100K each financial year. Oh, and we mustn't forget that it cost us £10K to install the three payment machines in the loos in the first place.'

Although Rob had dealt with initial complaints when the toilet closures were originally announced, they were part of a much bigger picture and he hadn't been aware of their specific operating costs at that time. He could hardly believe what he was hearing from Albert because it seemed incredible that three public lavatories would cost so much to operate.

Albert hadn't quite finished his lecture,

'As I've already said, we got a lot of grief when we shut down the other seven loos that we operated across the District, but try asking the Gazette if they can think of a way of subsidising that number with all the reductions we've had to make to our running costs. And just remember, Rob, providing lavs is not a statutory requirement - we could legitimately get away with scrapping them all if we desired. There would be no comebacks from Whitehall because it is not our legal duty to offer public lavatories. Just have a chat with Meera Chopra if you want confirmation.'

Rob was scratching his head trying to frame a response to Lena that encapsulated what Albert said with a good deal of softening around the edges,

'Have you any tips as to how I should respond to the Gazette, Albert?'

'Between you and me, I would tell them to piss off, which seems highly appropriate given the lavatorial context. Failing that, I suggest you consult the Cabinet Member for the Environment to see if he can offer a milder retort.'

The relevant Cabinet Member, Cllr Ron McGrath, was not the sharpest knife in the WDC box and, when Rob called him, the Councillor advised a preliminary response that was a good deal ruder than Albert's pithy rebuke. When pushed for a more diplomatic reply, Ron recommended *a good old fashioned no comment* stonewall approach, despite Rob's observation that WDC would be crucified all over again unless they offered a plausible explanation.

Undeterred, Rob decided to approach the Chair of the Council, Cllr Keith Wharton, in the hope that he might be persuaded to address the issue more constructively, in keeping with his statesman-like role. Keith's Labourite colleague, Cllr Dave Dillon, would have been the more obvious port of call given that he was the Cabinet Member for Health and Wellbeing but Rob knew from experience that *Red Dave*, as he was known to WDC officers, had been opposed to the cuts in services at the outset and would probably enjoy raking up his original reservations.

When Rob dialled Cllr Wharton's number his wife answered and asked Rob whether the call was absolutely necessary because her husband had not feeling well since his exertions at the ball. Rob was deeply apologetic and was about to terminate the conversation when the Council Chairman came on the line and told him not to worry about his spouse who was overreacting *as per usual.*

They spoke for a few minutes about the toilet dilemma, and this resulted in an agreed response that was a slight improvement on the previous iterations from Albert and Ron. Rob could tell that Keith's voice was fading fast as the dialogue progressed, and he rang off as soon as the official business was concluded. He then consulted the Legal Adviser and the Head of Democratic Services before providing Lena with a form of words that didn't upset the *Purdah* apple cart,

'Hi Lena. I've managed to get that quote you were chasing. You can attribute it to a WDC official spokesperson if you want to use it.'

'Good stuff, Rob. Fire away - my pen is poised.'

'OK. Here goes: *At WDC we strive to ensure that residents in our community can access facilities that support their health and wellbeing. For this reason, although it is not a legal requirement, we have continued to provide several lavatories for public use, despite the ongoing need to reduce our running costs whenever possible. Bearing in mind that the income from the use of WCs only covers about 15% of their overall cost, a majority of Councillors voted to reduce the number of facilities available last year. The decision was not taken lightly but was deemed necessary in light of the need to maintain expenditure on essential mandatory services. We still retain two toilet blocks in Woldchester and one in Titbury, and continue to keep the situation under review.* I hope that's enough to keep you happy for now.'

Lena thanked Rob sarcastically for his *stuffed shirt* spiel, but at least he had the satisfaction of knowing that his text was objective and relayed the Council's concerns about expenditure in a polite manner. He was 99.9% sure that Ric Sharkey was behind the antics of the *Phantom Urinator*, and wondered what other mischief he was planning to ensure victory in the forthcoming by-election.

Chapter XX

Vandal Scandal

As a rule, Meera Chopra's mother never contacted her when she was in her office at Reilly Road. That was why the Legal Advisor was so concerned when her mobile phone trilled and her frenzied Maa was on the end of the call, raving about her father being in distress. Meera immediately went into panic mode,

'Oh my gosh, Maa, has Pita had another heart attack? No - forget I said that. Don't break the news to me like this. I don't think I could stand it.'

'No no Meera, your father's old ticker is fine - he's just been shaken up a little ...but his pride has been hurt a lot and you must come quickly to the shop. Some boys have run riot and they have made a bit of a mess. Pita is having a lie down and he's asking to see you.'

Meera rang off promptly and pleaded with her Legal Services colleagues to cover a couple of urgent matters in her diary. She explained that she had to assist with an important family matter and they were very understanding when she provided a brief account of the unprovoked vandalism. As she set off for the store in East Titbury she reflected that her two brothers - a doctor and a teacher - also lived and worked within easy reach, but her mother would never have asked them to interrupt their important jobs and assist the family in its time of need!

She drove a good deal faster than normal and arrived at the corner shop that she knew so well from her younger days. While she was parking her BMW a few yards down the road, she was surprised to see that a sizeable huddle of people had gathered on the pavement to gawp at the scene of the crime. Glass was strewn around and someone had spray painted *Kil Aisian Invadors* across the threshold. When she approached the shop entrance, she recognised a familiar figure on the periphery of the group of onlookers and stopped in her tracks. Although he was trying to disguise his presence by wearing dark glasses and a baseball cap pulled down over most of his ugly features, there was no mistaking Horsfield. Meera resolved to march right up to him and call him out,

'Ah, Cllr Horsfield - oh, sorry it's just Mr Horsfield now isn't it? What brings you to this particular part of town?'

Horseface had tried to avoid her, but was forced to respond because the people on the pavement were all looking at him and expecting a reaction,

'Just er slumming, you know? Doing a bit of shopping here and there and I came across this unhappy scene. Disgusting I call it. What can you do with young lads these days? We should bring back national service to sort them out. Teach them some discipline and keep the little tinkers off the streets.'

'How did you know it was young boys? No, don't answer that - they're obviously not girls because they don't know how to spell, and I don't really care about them much whatever sex they may be. I'm much more interested in finding out if anyone was masterminding their efforts. Now he's the one who really deserves punishment. Don't you agree?'

'Well, now you're assuming that it was a male who was telling them what to do.'

'Oh, I know for sure that it was a man - or, to be more accurate, I would say an apology for a man.'

'You know, your lot are too clever by half - you should watch what you say.'

Meera tried to keep her cool,

'Mr Horsfield, what do you mean by *my lot* - kindly explain please.'

'You know, immigrants and the like who shouldn't be here in the first place.'

Some of the people at the scene overheard the conversation and didn't like the direction it was taking. A rather burly man in a tight fitting T-shirt and jogging pants advanced towards Horsfield and said,

'Hey, chap, leave it out! We've been shopping at Mr Chopra's for over twenty years and he and his wife are good mates. They even open on Christmas Day if we need to nip in for bits and pieces like batteries for toys and extra cans of booze.'

Horsfield got the message loud and clear, and Meera couldn't see his scrawny backside for dust when he realised that he might be cruising for a bruising. She thanked the tough guy - a loyal customer who she remembered serving in her youth - and then went indoors to comfort her parents.

Fortunately, the damage she encountered was mostly superficial and had been caused by a couple of young tearaways in hoodies. They had waited for a lull in footfall and had then overturned several display units and hurled a few tins of beans at the shop window, giving rise to a shower of glass across the pavement outside. When Meera's father had tried to intervene, they had manhandled him and inflicted a few cuts and bruises. None of his bones had been broken but Pita's self esteem was in tatters. He was sitting on a chair in his pyjamas and drinking green tea when Meera greeted him. Pita gave her a weak smile of recognition and said,

'Look at me, my precious daughter, I'm too old to take on two weedy teenagers! The CCTV is no bloody good because you can't see their faces, and the police have already visited and were no use whatsoever - all they did was issue an incident number. What is this world coming to eh?'

Meera consoled him and said softly,

'Don't fret Pita, Maa and I will see to the broken glass and there's some duct tape on the shelf over there that will be good enough to patch up the window until we get it repaired properly.'

'Thankyou, my little pearl. Tell me, Meera, why would anyone want to do this to us? We get shoplifters every now and again, but it's been years since we had any violence.'

'I have a good idea about who is behind this Pita, and I will find a way to stop him doing any more harm to us.'

Her father seemed reassured by her vow, but Meera had no idea how she was going to fulfil it. She knew that the police would not be interested in her suspicions about Horsfield's shenanigans without solid evidence of his involvement. As a lawyer, her only known advantage was her experience in file bashing, and she endeavoured to research the inner workings of the Woldshire Home Independence Party with a view to uncovering a possible chink in the armour of its creator.

Chapter XXI

Viv's verve vanishes

As expected, the revival of the toilet saga in the local press added an extra layer of dirt to the reputation of the Coalition regime, and a snap survey of voting preferences in South Titbury showed that the Lib Dem by-election candidate - a retired civil servant called Will Rafferty - would struggle to gather a modest amount of votes. The Conservative candidate, Wayne Kerr, was a handsome young devil who earned his living as an IT entrepreneur. Although he was nothing like the previous ward incumbent as far as appearances were concerned, Wayne claimed that he espoused many of the loathsome Horsfield's bigoted principles, and the Tory cognoscenti believed instinctively that his hardline rhetoric would be well received by a good number of householders in the locality.

Even the more moderate voters in South Titbury were not overly sympathetic towards the Coalition at WDC because they believed that their town had been neglected over the years. Their biggest grievance concerned the botched relocation of the County Council headquarters. A Conservative administration had planned to relocate County Hall from Woldchester to a brand new premises in South Titbury when it became clear that the old headquarters required a very costly refurbishment to remain fit for purpose. Contractors had already started preliminary work on the project when the Lib Dems gained control of the County Council, and the new leadership team - including Jim Harvey - cancelled the move.

The incoming regime opted to mothball a wing of the existing Woldchester HQ instead, with the intention of eventually renting it to new incumbents. They then commissioned a moderately priced upgrade to the remaining parts of the building and, as a result, Titbury was scarred by an abandoned construction site. The eyesore, complete with a surrounding chain link fence, was still in evidence two years on - a daily reminder for many residents of the perfidy of the Lib Dems.

Thanks to the tireless efforts of *The Shark's* worker bees, and the legacy of the abandoned building site in Titbury, it was little wonder that the Lib Dems were bracing themselves for a good thrashing in the by-election. Rob reflected that they had no answer to the Tory election machine and, despite his dislike for Cllr Sharkey, he was impressed by the man's burgeoning political nous. The campaign that Ric's team was conducting was little short of brilliant, and the only risk to his party securing a handsome victory was complacency. Ric was well aware of this potential banana skin and was working himself to a standstill to make sure that they would avoid any slips.

It was obvious that the Lib Dems were virtually writing off their chances of success in South Titbury days in advance of the vote because they didn't even bother delaying the announcement of redundancies at Reilly Road. Viv Bushby had offered to hold off for a while until the ballot had taken place, but Jim Harvey was conscious of the ultra high stress levels across the workforce and decided to bite the bullet as soon as he could.

Rob had already been tipped off by Jim personally that his own job was safe, but young Ozzie was less fortunate. The writing was on the wall when the lad received a phone call from Human Resources, inviting him to attend a consultation, and Ozzie already knew what to expect. Despite their love-hate relationship, Rob was saddened that his junior would be shown the door and he calculated that his redundancy deal would be rather modest taking account of his short time in post. It also dawned on Rob that all the chores carried out by Ozzie would now fall to him, which meant that he would be taking home the same salary while assuming a raft of extra responsibilities, including media monitoring, website updates, photocopying, photography, and tea making!

Rob expected Ozzie to be very downcast when he returned from his visit to HR but the lad was unexpectedly perky when asked how he was faring,

'Not three bad, Mr Boss Man. I've got four months worth of pay coming my way and that should be enough to buy my way into a start-up business that my mate Gibbo is launching. We're going to offer memorable experiences to punters and we think it will be a surefire winner. As an added extra, we've also got the band to fall back on, and we're beginning to rack up a few more bookings for functions around the county. That charity ball gig did us a lot of good - we're going great guns now and we're charging more as well to make it much more worthwhile.'

Rob began to suspect that Ozzie had actually welcomed the chop, and when he enquired more about his erstwhile colleague's new venture with his pal, the lad replied enthusiastically,

'Gifts are naff these days for most folk - they're hardly ever what people really want and a lot of them end up in charity shops. Gibbo reckons that lots of punters are far more interested in doing stuff and creating memories. You know the sort of thing I mean: balloon rides; chauffeur-driven limos; luxury hotel breaks; residential master classes for cookery or arty crafty stuff; visits to restaurants with seven course tasting menus. You get the drift?'

Rob was genuinely amazed by Ozzie's positive demeanour and had never seen him so animated when talking about his career prospects. It had been plain for a long while that the youngster had not been over keen on his role in the Council and he was now behaving like a felon released from death row. Turning to Rob, he added,

'Once we're up and running Rob, I'll give you a generous discount if you fancy booking a romantic wine tasting weekend with a certain young lady who seems to be warming towards you for some unaccountable reason.'

Rob thanked him for his generous offer and hoped that the relationship with Sandy would gravitate towards the level that Ozzie envisaged.

Elsewhere in Reilly Road, most members of staff who were being let go were less sanguine when they heard the news. The union rep, Doug Davies, was flitting around the building consoling the officers who had received the call from HR, and reminded them that he had done his best in extremely trying circumstances. The redundancy packages he had negotiated were at the higher end of the scale and he was convinced that he had secured the best deal possible - but he knew that many workers were experiencing the equivalent of a kick in the guts, and he hated this part of his job.

Despite Doug's sterling efforts, he was verbally abused by a handful of demoralised officers who were lashing out at him, purely and simply because he was an easy target. Those who had escaped the noose were also not too pleased because - like Rob - they knew that they would have to graft even harder to keep on top of punishing workloads.

Reilly Road had lost several experienced hands through a previous redundancy programme and, since then, the HR team had managed to reduce numbers on the payroll more humanely by not always replacing every member of staff who had resigned or retired. That tactic was effective up to a point until the Covid pandemic caused a spate of resignations when older officers got fed up with home working and decided to leave the world of work forever. This in turn removed any remaining room for flexibility in managing the Council's staffing numbers while retaining its full range of services. In other words, the new wave of staff cuts meant that some functions would discontinue and public dissatisfaction would increase.

Viv Bushby ensured that she was available throughout the day should anyone want to chat with her, but nobody took advantage of her offer. She realised that the challenge of achieving culture change through Roger Pitt's *Future Journey* programme was now even more daunting, but she trusted that a sufficient number of mature adults left on the payroll would concede that effective joint working with West Fordham was the only way forward in view of the perilous financial picture within both authorities.

She knew that nearly every council across the country was in the same position as WDC, due largely to the fact that their largest overhead was people. It wasn't just the salary costs either. The relatively generous staff pension schemes set up in consultation with the unions during the *fat years* - when public services were better funded - were coming back to haunt most local authorities. Despite the harsh revisions that had been made to the pension provisions for more recent joiners, the old stagers were reaping the benefits of long service when they hung up their boots.

Realising that she had been snubbed by the staff big time, Viv followed Doug's lead and walked around the building to make herself visible to everyone, and tried in vain to comfort some of the officers who had been released. Some warmed to her efforts while others blatantly ignored her. Whatever their opinion of her as a Chief Exec, Viv was clearly upset at the prospect of parting company with so many loyal and valued workers. and she shed a few tears back in her room when the wretched day was coming to a close.

She was just about to pack up for the evening when her mobile pinged and she flicked open the screen to reveal a message that reduced the day's events to a mere sideshow. It was a brief note from the son of Cllr Keith Wharton informing her that his father had suffered a massive stroke earlier that day and - after a long wait for an ambulance - had died on his way to hospital.

Chapter XXII

NOC knocking on the door...

Achieving victory in the by-election in the South Titbury ward - to fill the vacancy left by Charles Horsfield - was a massive priority for *The Shark* as it would ensure the Conservatives reached the magical number of 16 seats on the Council. He knew that an expected win for his man Wayne Kerr would result in a further weakening of the Coalition's hold on power. But the biggest plus from Ric's viewpoint was that it would reinforce WDC's status as a NOC (No Overall Control) council, a term commonly used to describe a local authority in which no party had an overall majority.

Ric was savouring the prospect of capturing Charles's seat but he simply couldn't believe the twist of fate when the news came through about Cllr Wharton's demise, paving the way to the possible overthrow of the entire Coalition regime at Reilly Road. Now that a winnable Labour ward was also up for grabs, the Tories had high hopes of boosting their total to 17 seats, which would leave the Lib Dems with 16 and a sole Labour ally, Cllr Dave Dillon, weighing in with one. Ric calculated that he would then be able to take over the leadership of the Council courtesy of the Tories being the biggest party!

Unlike Keith Wharton, Cllr *Dave The Red* Dillon had been less inclined to get into bed with the Lib Dems even though he was kept at bay through the award of a Cabinet post in the Coalition. It was debatable whether he would continue to cooperate with Jim Harvey's team so readily now that his senior colleague had kicked the bucket. Dave was appalled when Cllr Wharton didn't nominate a Labour candidate to fight the by-election in South Titbury, and he was determined that they wouldn't roll over a second time when East Woldchester was up for grabs.

Jim Harvey was depressed enough about the almost certain defeat for the Lib Dems in South Titbury, but he was devastated when he contemplated the possibility of voters switching from Labour to the Tories in East Woldchester. Fearing the worst, he called yet another meeting with his Cabinet colleagues and assessed the local political *zeitgeist*,

'I think we all agree that Charles Horsfield's ward is lost for all intents and purposes. The vote is coming up soon and our man Will Rafferty has a snowball's chance in Hell given the way things are going down there. I did some canvassing with him the other day and I got double egged all over my best suit as soon as we hit the first street on our rounds.

He paused and passed a copy of a glossy Tory leaflet around the table,

'Just to cap it all, this little bombshell is circulating around the Ward. The headline is a bit blunt but says it all really: *Vote Conservative if you don't want a Piss Poor Council!* They're running rings around us, and there's not a lot we can do. You know, Will Rafferty's a good guy and takes all the hostility in his stride, but the poor sod's always on the back foot as soon as he knocks on doors, and he can't land any punches because we're such a tainted brand across the whole area.'

Cllr Tom Anderson, the Cabinet Member for Customer and Regulatory Services, was equally downcast,

'We're not just getting it in the neck in South Titbury though are we, Jim? I don't think we're the flavour of the month anywhere at the moment. And that leaflet is obviously piggybacking on the fresh criticism about the cuts in toilet provision. We got hammered for it when we did the deed last year and now we're getting a second helping of angst from the disabled lobby.'

Environment Cabinet Member Cllr McGrath added,

'Yep, I know from experience that the loos are the gift that keeps on giving for the Tories. Rob Cummings sent his news digest around this morning and one of the items said that Sharkey is now pushing for us to install more accessible toilets across the whole district. There's a big spread in the Examiner about him going around Woldchester with an old dear in a wheelchair who can't get into either of the public conveniences that are still operating. And that's not the worst of it. The Gazette has a feature about the leisure centre we closed down in Titbury and stresses that it had excellent accessible WC facilities - they've even included a photo of the loos gathering dust with Cllr Ashurst standing in the foreground looking as cross as crabs.'

Health and Well Being portfolio holder Cllr *Dave the Red* Dillon decided it was time to add his Socialist five pennorth,

'I warned you all about the harmful effects of reducing the number of toilet blocks but you wouldn't listen. I know it costs a packet to provide lavs but we're fast becoming a zombie organisation that is only fit to empty the bins, manage election processes and assess planning applications. People deserve better than that - especially the disabled.'

Cllr Hilley, the Planning Committee Chair, interjected and said,

'Dave, we've all gone over this ground before. Those closures were absolutely necessary to keep our heads above water. There wasn't an alternative - and you ought to know that. You saw the spreadsheets just like everybody else.'

At that point, Cllr Dillon got up from his chair and left the room in high dudgeon, telling the others that he had better things to do than being told to abandon the principles that he had espoused for forty five years by endorsing harmful cuts to services.

Jim Harvey bowed his head in submission, and groaned,

'Oh deep joy - I realise that our colleague is upset about Keith dying but I hope he's not going to chuck all of his toys out of the pram.'

Cllr McGrath was equally despondent,

'Dave was never really onside with any of the service reductions, and Keith Wharton just about kept him in line until he snuffed it. Now that his pal's not with us any more we can't rely on Dave for support. It's obvious that Cllr Sharkey's remarks about the lack of toilet provision for disabled residents have touched a raw nerve as far as Dave's concerned, and it's going to be difficult to entice our Socialist ally back into the fold.'

Jim agreed and ventured a feeble joke,

'I dare say that the Tories will be *flushed with success* on this one and I have an inkling that they might be putting more of our cuts under the microscope over the next few days to see if they can put a fresh negative spin on them.'

He then continued in a spirited tone,

'Come on, though, let's start looking at the positives. Despite all this negativity in the papers, I still think we should be able to win a lot of converts in East Woldchester. Even though Keith was a popular chap, he didn't have a large majority and we ran him close last time. The Tories finished a poor third if I remember correctly.'

Cllr Hilley interjected,

'Jim, you're forgetting that they lost a lot of votes to one of Horsfield's WHIP fanatics - and the Tories will probably pick up more support if there isn't a strong independent in the running. We'll have to wait and see what happens on the WHIP front, but their guy from the last time around went to jail for child pornography offences last year, and it's debatable whether Horsfield will be able to dredge up another fascist clown to take his place - especially if critics start digging up the trench debacle again. '

Cllr McGrath groaned at the inadvertent pun and then tried to put things in perspective,

'Look, we shouldn't really be too concerned about what WHIP might or might not do anyway. What we really need, gentlemen, is a charismatic candidate of our own who appeals to a broad range of voters. Answers on a postcard!'

A similar gathering was taking place in Ric Sharkey's little enclave further up the corridor. He could sense the hands of destiny on his shoulders and found it hard to be too sombre when talking about the late Cllr Wharton,

'I think we all agree that Keith was a nice bloke and I've already called his widow to tell her that the Conservative Party is sorry to hear of her loss. But life, as they say, goes on and we have this fantastic opportunity to seize the day if we're hungry enough. I can safely say that South Titbury is in the bag and I actually think we can build on that success and spring a surprise in East Woldcheste, provided we get our act together.'

Cllr Lesley Ashurst was equally bubbly,

'It's a tough ask, Ric, but I've already lined up some of our best social media influencers to talk up the benefits of voting Tory in Keith's old ward. We're already stoking up more dissatisfaction with the Coalition's policies and we'll keep on looking for new angles to exploit, just like we did with the loos.'

Grant Lewis, the Tory Councillor in the ward bordering East Woldchester, was less enthusiastic,

'That's all well and good, Lesley, but we can't keep reheating old stuff. If we want to make a big impression in Keith's old stamping

162

ground, we need to highlight something fresh as well. Is there anything out there that might do the trick?'

RIc and Lesley exchanged glances and both smiled simultaneously.

Meanwhile in her London penthouse apartment, Nadine Hurley was also digesting the latest news about the death of Cllr Wharton and the possibilities that it might bring. She was lying on the sofa in a state of partial undress while Joe Baxter - the *Dyno Interactive* whizz kid - busied himself in the kitchen preparing an omelette for two, clad only in electric blue boxer shorts.

They were celebrating another new contract for Joe, this time a moderately successful courier company. The firm intended to keep its drivers on their toes by monitoring their activities more closely through a motion-sensitive device hooked up to the dashboards in their vans. Joe was in a great mood and had brought gifts of champagne and chocolates for the delectable Ms Hurley, who returned the favour by treating him to a strenuous afternoon of love making. They were old friends and often met up when he had business in the Capital and fancied sharing a warm bed for the night.

As Joe whisked eggs furiously, Nadine remained in a state of post-climax bliss, and contemplated the sweet possibility of the Conservatives taking over at WDC. She flicked through the messages on her mobile and called through to Joe,

'I can't make our theatre date next week, Joey darling. Things are hotting up in Woldchester and I want to be at the heart of our campaign to gain control of the Council. RIc has asked me to supervise the team and it's going to be sooo epic.'

Joe was less than impressed,

'Off to hold his hand again eh? I honestly don't know why you bother with that irritating wimp. He's a nasty little piece of work in terms of his likeability, if you want my opinion.'

'Well I don't, so don't go there. Ric's a twit of the first order but he's always eager to please when I'm around and he can't help it if he lacks a personality. I've been grooming him for a long time now and it's incredible that I've almost hit the jackpot. My uncle will be absolutely delighted if we gain control of the Council and you'll do okay as well.'

Joe stopped whisking and looked up,

'You mean that I might still get the nod for the *Dyno Interactive* contract at WDC? It's been a while since I made my pitch and the direction of traffic hasn't been good - the pillocks never even reciprocated my interest in terms of calls.'

'Absolutely. If RIc takes over and calls the shots, I'm sure he'll be able to nod your proposals through. You know, Joey boy, he actually likes you - because when you turn on the charm, you're almost irresistible, even to automatons like Ric.'

'Well it's a good job that he doesn't know about us. I don't think he'd be so well disposed to interfacing with me then would he?'

Having said that, Joe noticed that Nadine had risen from the sofa and was moving towards him with a rapacious look in her eye, peeling off what remained of her clothes as she advanced across the floor. She hastily swept aside the contents of the kitchen table and said,

'Forget the omelette, Joeykins. Let's get down and dirty in the kitchen, you naughty little boy.'

Chapter XXIII

Flying the flag

With two by-elections looming, the annual Armed Forces Day flag raising event at Reilly Road took on an added significance for WDC councillors, and quite a few took advantage of being seen at a public gathering to laud heroes past and present. In normal circumstances, the Chair of the Council would have done the honours at a meagre ceremony attended by a few British Legion veterans, a handful of WDC officers (including Rob who doubled as a photographer), the odd member of the public and another token councillor or two.

On this occasion - owing to the passing of Cllr Wharton - the local Tory MP, Sir Cedric Phillips, agreed to step into the breach and delivered a short speech praising the contribution of service personnel. It was the first time that the MP had attended the gathering and he was astounded to see such a good turn out. The massed ranks of councillors drawn from the Lib Dem/Labour Coalition and Conservative Party were very much in evidence, together with a horde of WDC officers, a large crowd of onlookers, and reporters from a good selection of local and regional newspapers. However, the Jewel in the Crown was the appearance of an Armoured Personnel Carrier from Titbury Barracks, carrying five squaddies in dress uniform. To complete the picture, Sandy turned up at the last minute with the six Combined Cadet Force students who had nearly come to grief in Horsfield's ditch when they had been drilling there a couple of weeks earlier.

A patch of earth with grass seed scattered on it was all that now remained of the ill-starred dugout, and Stan Seymour had taken care to remove the hazard warning tape around the plot to make sure that it didn't detract from the spectacle. Nevertheless, several people were lining up to take photographs of the newly dug plot so that they could exhibit some *before* and *after* montages.

Sandy had confessed to Rob previously that she wanted to take the kids back to the scene of the near disaster so that they could all create some pleasant memories of the flag ceremony with a view to banishing any lingering trauma. She made eye contact with him on her arrival, and also nodded in his direction when the cadets lined up alongside the serving soldiers to hear Sir Cedric deliver the speech that Rob had prepared for Cllr Wharton a few weeks earlier.

The oration focused on a thankyou letter from a young girl to a British soldier who had rescued her from a collapsed building in Sierra Leone. The tone wasn't as jingoistic as the veteran parliamentarian would have liked, but Sir Cedric was delighted when it appeared to go down well with his audience and he was happy to milk the applause that followed. He then gave the signal for Stan Seymour to raise the flag and took the salute from the military personnel, British Legion veterans and CCF cadets.

Rob glanced around at the members of the public present and noticed that one person looked very familiar but he couldn't quite place him. He concentrated harder and it eventually came to him that he was viewing a spruced up version of the hero of the hour,

Fred Clark, who was wearing a rather snazzy suit that made him look very distinguished. He had arrived unannounced and was standing on the periphery to avoid any fuss or bother. However, Fred's efforts at self effacement were in vain because some people in the crowd recognised him instantly and insisted on him gaining a better view of the proceedings. In doing so, he managed to spot the small teenage girl that he had rescued from the flood and her face was a picture of glee when he winked at her.

Rob thought it was highly ironic that the ceremony had been enhanced considerably because of *Horseface's* tireless efforts and yet he was nowhere to be seen. At least he thought that was the case until he caught sight of a familiar mournful figure peering through the bushes. The hidden architect of the extravaganza witnessed the proceedings from afar and no doubt wished that he could be centre stage receiving plaudits for his efforts.

When the ceremony was over, Sir Cedric' aide didn't want him to be upstaged by Fred Clark, so he made a point of instructing his boss to shake the latters' hand firmly and ensure that the media hacks took photos of the two of them together. Once he had done with the local hero, the MP was steered towards a group huddle with Ric Sharkey and his minions to review the progress of both by-election campaigns. Sir Cedric seemed well pleased with Ric's upbeat report and then his aide made their excuses to leave, claiming an urgent need for the MP to attend an important vote in the House of Commons.

Fred was a reluctant star guest but he warmed to the task and clearly enjoyed talking to the young cadets, including the two that he had pulled out of the trench. He also made a point of seeking out the Chair of the Planning Committee , Cllr Hilley, to thank him for reconvening the abandoned Council meeting, resulting in the approval of the application to build affordable homes in Little Chipping, including a large new family home for the Craig/Clark clan.

The Chief Exec's PA, Maria Milburn, hadn't expected such a large crowd and was rushing hither and thither to prepare extra teas, coffees and soft drinks for the guests. She had dispatched a colleague to the shops for more biscuits and was waiting anxiously for her return because the stocks were dwindling fast.Rob was busy helping her dole out snacks and drinks but he kept his eyes peeled for a sight of Sandy again and his patience was rewarded when she tapped him on the shoulder and begged a quick coffee before she herded the teenagers back to school.

While she was drinking, Rob whispered to her,

'I had a great time the other night, Sand. Are you and me still on for the cinema tomorrow?'

'Of course we are, silly boy. I've been looking forward to it. Now go and serve more tea and biccies to the hordes and let me get back to my life of drudgery in the classroom.'

She gave him a little peck on the cheek and then set off to round up her charges.

'Ooh, my. Looks like you're in there!' piped up Rob's junior colleague. Ozzie had been entertaining the veterans with tales about his new enterprise and had offered them all discounts on hot air balloon rides. He was in fine fettle and whispered to Rob,

'You've done alright for yourself this time, boss. Your girl looks a bit severe in her work clothes, but I've seen how well she scrubs up when she's out on the town, and she definitely has a bit of class about her.'

Rob took this as a seal of approval but he still felt the need to administer a verbal rap across the knuckles to his young assistant for the horribly sexist take on his burgeoning relationship with Sandy,

'You make her sound like a prize heifer at the Woldshire Show, Ozzie! But I suppose I get your drift.'

Meanwhile, Rob noticed that Fred Clark had been intercepted by Jim Harvey and that they were spending a long time deep in conversation. Rob didn't think any more of it until he was back at his desk later and Jim burst into his office like a kid in a candy store. Without pausing for breath, he ordered Rob to issue a media release as soon as possible,

'I know we're in *Purdah* and all that nonsense, but Meera says we're perfectly entitled to issue a factual statement, announcing that the Lib Dem candidate for the late Cllr Wharton's ward will be a certain Mr Frederick Clark!'

For the first time in a long while, Jim didn't look like a noose was tightening around his neck. Even though the outcome of the by-election in South Titbury would almost certainly be a Conservative gain, he now sensed that his party had a fighting chance of gaining a seat in East Woldchester, thus ensuring that the Lib Dems would retain control of the administration.

Chapter XXIV

Crafty car park chicanery

As her long working day was drawing to a close, Meera was exhausted after dealing with complaints from the Office of the Information Commissioner which took up her whole afternoon. The Commissioner was hauling the Council over the coals for the lack of timely responses to a ridiculously large amount of Freedom Of Information requests from the public. She suspected that many of them originated from cronies of Ric Sharkey but she had no way of proving it. Instead, she had pleaded that the avalanche of queries was proving too much for overworked and under-resourced staff but her appeals for clemency had not gone down too well on the other end of the phone.

Regardless, *The Shark* was the least of Meera's worries because she'd received two anonymous phone calls in quick succession during the course of the day, each advising her to *piss off back to your stinking hovel in India, you stupid bitch*. There were no prizes for guessing who was orchestrating such blatantly crude harassment - but again, she had no definite proof. Like Rob, she had spotted Horsfield's repulsive mug through the decorative bushes during the Armed Forces ceremony. She had been especially alarmed when he had stared at her and mimed slitting her throat before disappearing into the gloom again.

Meera's conviction about the identity of her anonymous telephone persecutor didn't prevent her from feeling deeply unsettled when she walked out of Reilly Road at dusk and entered the car park to reclaim her much loved BMW - one of the few perks of her job. She was just about to slide on to her comfy leather seat when she caught sight of an ugly scratch along the driver's side rear door. A further inspection also revealed that the front nearside tyre was as flat as a pancake. At that precise moment, Horsfield just happened to sidle up to her innocently, his face a picture of concern,

'Oh dear, oh dear Ms Chopra. It looks like someone's taken exception to you driving a big flash car. What a real shame, my dear. Must have been some hooligans I reckon.'

Meera was outraged on hearing his faux sympathy and shouted at him,

'It was you, you steamin' great idiot! How dare you interfere with my car!! Look at the damage you've done, you.. you fuckin' imbecile!'

'That's a very serious allegation, especially from the mouth of a qualified lawyer eh? It's a good job I've activated the voice recorder on my mobile because I've got some pretty good evidence when I sue you for slander.'

'I can't believe I'm hearing this. You harass and bully me and now you've got the nerve to claim that you're the victim! Hah - that really takes the cake.. with extra chocolate sprinkles on top!'

Despite her defiant tone, Meena realised that the crazy zealot had the upper hand, and her heart sank when he concluded,

'Listen Ms Chopra. I've switched off the recorder now so we can speak in confidence. If you want all this misery to go away, all you have to do is clear out of this country and take your whole stinking family with you. There's plenty more tricks up my sleeves if you

171

choose to hang around, so I would suggest that you all go now if you know what's good for you.'

Meera was stunned when confronted by such pure hatred and bowed her head in despair because she didn't know what to say in return. Then the ensuing silence was harshly interrupted by another voice that sounded vaguely familiar.

'I actually know what's good for Meera. And it isn't what you have in mind, you manky little turd.'

Looking up, she noticed that the Reilly Road maintenance man Stan Seymour had crept up on them from behind, clutching a large baseball bat.

Horsfield was rather perturbed when Stan showed up, but he regained his composure swiftly and tried to maintain control of the situation,

'Mr Seymour, please return to your post. This is a private matter between me and Ms Chopra. She defamed me and I intend to take legal action to clear my name. Now leave us alone and be on your way.'

Stan gave a brief half smile and replied,

'I've never liked you and your sly ways, Horsfield. Harassing a woman on her own is very much your style isn't it? There's something you ought to know before you start wailing about defamation or other claptrap. You see, after the flood in the car park - caused by your ridiculous trench, by the way - the Health and Safety inspector told me to install more CCTV cameras around the site so that I would be able to monitor things better. Now if you look at the top of the lamp post just behind you, you'll see the little beauty that we activated yesterday.'

As instructed, Horsfield raised his gaze to the sky and was greeted by the appearance of a discrete white box with a protruding lens. He - and also Meera - took in the new addition to the security infrastructure while Stan resumed his narrative,

'I didn't expect the new gizmo to prove its worth on its maiden voyage, but I'm pleased to say that it's passed with flying colours - that means I've managed to get some decent footage of what happened here before Meera came to reclaim her vehicle.'

Stan elaborated,
'I was busy scanning the screens to see if they were all working properly and I noticed that a certain pathetic loser was damaging Meera's car and then he jumped behind a wall to lie in wait for her.'

The colour drained out of the culprit's face and he tried to reason with his fellow former comrade in arms,

'Hey, Stan old son, as one old soldier to another, how about we forget this whole damn thing eh? You fought for your country and so did I - we both wanted to make sure that it was a better place for everyone who belongs here.'

'That's right, chum. Everyone who belongs here, including our Meera here. She and her family are a terrific example of how to integrate successfully into the neighbourhood. I wouldn't mind betting that they contribute a hell of a lot more to our future prosperity than you and your skanky little WHIP bully boys.'

Meera blushed when her family was mentioned in a favourable light, but remained silent as Stan proceeded with his rant,

'I'm not a man of violence by nature, *Horseface*. I've seen too much of it on my tours of duty in Northern Ireland. Even so, I can make the odd exception and it wouldn't take much for me to ram this here bat up your weedy little toy soldier arse. And if you dare to venture anywhere near Meera in the future, I've got some handy CCTV footage that might help the police with their enquiries, matey. I take it that you also wouldn't want my evidence to come to light if you dared to sue Meera for defamation?'

Horsfield knew that the game was up, and he didn't respond to Stan's aggressive taunts. He was preparing to withdraw with a shred of his dignity intact when the maintenance man chirped up again,

'Before you go, sunshine, I think we've got some admin to look after. Now I reckon that the damage you inflicted on that high-end car is going to cost a fair amount of money. I've got a pal in the trade and he can probably sort it out for about five hundred quid cash. I'll inflate the flat tyre myself as a gesture of goodwill. You can't say fairer than that, eh?'

Although he was skewered, Horsfield was reluctant to comply,

'Come on, Stan. Where am I going to get that sort of spare cash at short notice?'

Meera at last saw a chance to intervene,

174

'Well, one of the things I'm allowed to do in my job is the investigation of certain financial fraud dealings, some of which may be of interest to the National Crime Agency. I've started to review your WHIP records and I'm not at liberty to tell you about my findings. Let's just say that potential discrepancies might warrant further investigation. And I'm not talking about one or two pennies turning up down the back of your sofa, Mr Horsfield.'

Charles looked a tad worried when she brought up the *F word* in the monetary sense, and he remained tight-lipped as she elaborated,

'It's not all bad news for you on the money front. I also noticed that you're due quite a few allowance payments for attending Council and Committee meetings - that's a good start if you want to turn up some legitimate funds quickly. I'll do you a favour and have a word with the Finance team to see if they can expedite the payments. That means you'll have plenty of money available very soon to pay for the damage to my car.'

Stan was jubilant,

'Problem solved about the readies then...now we're cooking with gas eh? Okay, then, my weedy friend, I know where you live so I'll come around to your place tomorrow night for the folding stuff. Oh, and by the way, I'll bring my panel beater pal to make sure there's no funny business. He's a lot tougher than me - used to be in the Marines - so he doesn't need a baseball bat if he wants to give someone a good leathering.'

Horsfield acknowledged his agreement to the arrangements soundlessly with a slight nod of the head, and then made his exit at speed, probably because he needed to change his Y-fronts. When he was almost out of earshot he attempted a feeble show of defiance and yelled,

'Traitors like you are playing into the hands of these foreign freeloaders, Seymour. Some of the local Tories here are cottoning on to the threat and I bet you'll change your mind about immigrants one day - just you wait and see.''

Stan shouted back,

'Aye,chum, maybe when Hell freezes over!'

He then turned to Meera and noticed that she was shaking like a blancmange. As tears began to roll down her face, Stan offered her a newly ironed handkerchief and said softly,

'It's all over now, dear. He might be a stupid little shit, but he's still got enough sense to back off and stay away from you for good.'

Meera was almost overcome with relief and expressed her profuse gratitude in an outpouring of emotion,

'How can I thank you enough, Stan? Tha.. that man was trying to ruin my life - and, you know what, he was also using his spotty young hooligans to menace my parents.'

'It's my pleasure, Meera. Little turds like *Horseface* don't know their Arsenals from their Evertons. He's not fit to tie your shoelaces, pet. As for his comments about Tory sympathisers - we'll just have to wait and see what gives but I doubt whether they'll do you any harm.''

Meera stopped crying and forced out a radiant smile as she declared joyously,

'I'm just so glad that the CCTV was installed in time and you caught him in the act.'

Stan almost convulsed when she made her remark and he replied,

'Oh, there's one thing that I forgot to mention to him ...that camera isn't wired up yet, and probably won't be up and running for at least another couple of days. It's a good job that *Horseface* wasn't smart enough to demand sight of the footage, isn't it?'

Meera was astounded,

'Oh my God!! You had me convinced completely, you fibber! But er tell me Stan, if you didn't have the camera to help you, how did you know that he was here?'

'Pure dumb luck really. I was locking up the portacabin to go home when I saw some movement in the bushes behind the car park - so I nipped back to my locker and grabbed the bat. I thought it might just be kids mucking about but I had this strange notion that our chum Charles might be on the prowl. Rob told me he was hanging around in there at the flag raising and I doubted whether we'd finally seen the back of the creepy bastard. Anyway, I waited in the shadows for a while and I hit the jackpot when I saw him jump out of his hiding place to damage your car and then skedaddle behind the wall before you arrived. I held back from doing anything until he'd made himself known to you and then I knew that I had to act straight away.'

'So, let's get this right, there's definitely no CCTV footage whatsoever showing Horsfield attacking my car? '

'Absolutely. Nada.... hey, what are you laughing at?'

'Well it's true what I said about him being due some attendance expenses but my spiel about financial fraud was a complete load of bullshit. I was dying to probe his grubby little WHIP set-up but I was told to go forth and multiply when I asked the National Crime Agency to investigate them. Judging by his reaction, though, Horsfield appears to have something to hide - he looked a bit green around the gills when I hinted at discrepancies in his party's funding didn't he?'

It was Stan's turn to gasp in admiration,

'And I thought I was the bee's knees when it came to bluffing! What can I say, Meera? You've completely blown me out of the water... and what a crafty touch to include something that was true to throw him off the scent. I tell you what, I wouldn't like to take you on at poker now I know you can keep such a straight face.'

Meera basked in the warmth of his flattery and confided with a grin,

'I think our talents for fabrication will have to remain our shared little secret just to make sure *Horseface* never gets wind of what we've been up to. We both gambled on him being gullible, but he might catch on through the rumour mill if we started bragging about pulling the wool over his eyes.'

'No problem on that score, Meera. Even the wife will not be privy to how we conned the chocolate warrior. Provided we both zip our lips, I don't think he'll be bothering you or your folks again.'

Chapter XXV

The final curtain call

Like many modern day funerals, the ceremony to mark the passing of former Cllr Keith Wharton was an extremely joyous occasion with mourners urged to wear bright colours and radiant smiles on their faces. Hundreds of people crammed into the Baptist Chapel in East Woldchester, including most members of the Council, a good number of WDC officers and the entire membership of the local amateur dramatic society. Keith had been much loved by his close family and the large turnout confirmed that he was also held in high regard within a wide range of social circles. As usual, most of the congregation only discovered his hidden depths - and the happiness he brought to so many others - during the course of the informative eulogy delivered by his son.

In his lifetime, Keith had accumulated an impressive list of achievements, and many of those paying their respects were genuinely astonished to learn that he had been very successful as a director and scriptwriter for the Woldchester Players for over forty years. He had also excelled as a swimming instructor, amateur footballer, competitive ballroom dancer, vegetable gardening fanatic and charity fundraiser. In fact, some of the local politicians in attendance wondered how Keith had found the time to serve as a Labour councillor!

As the service came to a close, a smart speaker blared out *Things can only get better* by D Ream, harking back to the heady days of the Blair administration before it all turned sour for Labour. The anthem was one of the very few elements of the funeral that had political overtones and it was enough to fire up the arch socialist Cllr Dave Dillon, who remarked to his wife,

'Look at all them sanctimonious Tory and Lib Dem creeps, love. They'll be fighting like cats and dogs soon to grab some votes in Keith's ward, but at least he's managed to shut their gobs for a short while.'

She wasn't really listening to him because she was fantasising about acquiring a wardrobe to match the stylish ensemble worn by Cllr Starkey's partner in the fifth pew down, rather than having to settle for the odd Per Una top in the M&S sales. Deep down, she had always hated Dave's class prejudices and craved a little more luxury in her drab life rather than being dragged along to tiresome rain-soaked protest marches that never seemed to change anything for the better.

As a mark of respect, all activities related to the two forthcoming by-elections had been suspended for the day and, after the ceremony, it was refreshing to see representatives from all parties engaging in friendly conversation about everyday matters. Even *The Shark* seemed to be trying his best to be civil, helped in large measure by the presence of the glamorous partner on his arm.

Being naturally gregarious, Nadine Hurley was in her element working the room, and she was gleefully conscious of the admiring looks she was attracting from several guests by virtue of her little black Versace dress and midnight blue Manolo Blahnik heels. Rob was not overly interested in her designer wardrobe, but he was racking his brains again to recall when he had first seen the woman, and he was frustrated when he couldn't dredge up the recollection.

Quite a few mourners moved on to a nearby hotel for snacks, drinks and cordial conversation, courtesy of the Wharton family, and senior WDC officers were reminded of how peaceful their lives used to be at Reilly Road when the ward members rubbed along together in spite of their ideological differences. Nadine continued to sparkle at the reception and served up a high wattage grin to everyone she encountered. She was mindful that she would be the Council's *First Lady* if the Tories managed to win both by-elections and she was desperate to make a good impression on the masses, especially after her untimely departure from the charity ball when Ric had made such a fool of himself after the auction.

Rob was at the buffet table chatting to the familiar newshounds Lena Montgomery and Tom Irwin.They had been dispatched to report on the occasion and were trying to snaffle a generous amount of drinks and eats in the process. As they munched away, he quizzed them,

'Why do I keep thinking I've seen Nadine Hurley in a different guise? I know she's a PR person in the city but I have a nagging suspicion that she has another string to her bow.'

Both had no idea about her potential alter ego existence, and didn't really seem to care much. Instead, Lena was happy to take a few snaps of Nadline's stylish costume to grace the society pages of the Gazette's *Woldshire People* supplement, and she then observed sharply,

'What on earth does a really attractive woman like her see in a twerp like Sharkey?'

Tom Irwin explained,

'Power can be a strong aphrodisiac, Lena. Ric might look like a pipsqueak but he could be destined for higher things the way he's shaping up, especially with such a good looking helpmate in tow. There are strong rumours that the local MP will hand over the reins to him further downstream and who knows how far he'll progress eventually.'

Rob suddenly had horrific visions of Sharkey rising to the rank of Chancellor of the Exchequer in a national government. He imagined him screwing up the whole country with his trademark forensic attention to futile financial issues, rather than just being content to mess with the efficient running of WDC. A gloomy Dave Dillon seemed to read Rob's mind when he ambled across to him and muttered,

'God help us when that wazzock gets to call the shots at Reilly Road. I haven't got much time for Jim Harvey and his munchkins but this guy is the antiChrist in comparison. Poor old Keith will be turning in his newly dug grave!'

Chapter XXVI

Fred fried for frolicking

The blessed hiatus from electioneering was only too brief and both major parties resumed hostilities the day after Keith Wharton was laid to rest. The Lib Dems - buoyed by the successful wooing of Fred

Clark as their candidate - were putting a lot of effort into their campaign in East Woldchester, and the reaction on doorsteps was proving to be largely positive.

Jim Harvey was in a buoyant frame of mind and convened his inner circle to deliver the favourable news,

'I'm not counting my chickens, guys, but it looks like we've backed the right horse this time and the Tory goose might be cooked.'

Cllr Tom Anderson, the portfolio holder for Customer and Regulatory Services, winced under the impact of a barrage of mixed metaphors but agreed with the sentiment expressed,

'I'm picking up good vibes as well. Fred's not a deep thinker by any means but he looks pretty damn good when he dolls himself up, and he's still dining out on his life saving exploits at Reilly Road.'

Neverthless, Tom still felt it was necessary to emphasise the gravity of the situation,

'Don't forget that we all have to stay alert and stop Fred from opening his mouth too much. He knows sod all about the finer points of our policies so we need to protect him from elephant trap questions at all times. The Tories manage to keep their local MP onside despite the pompous git not having much of a clue about his party's manifesto so it is do-able if we all muck in.'

The Cabinet Member for the Environment, Cllr McGrath added,

'What we must do now is double down on the heroism aspect. I think we all agree that Fred's our only hope of staying in power because South Titbury is looking like a complete non-starter for us... so no screw ups please, gentlemen.'

Although the Lib Dems were convinced that the Tories would be itching to exploit Fred's lack of political nous, unbeknown to them Team Sharkey had another strategy to deal with the new kid on the block. Ric summoned his acolytes and set out a cunning plan to undermine the *hero effect*,

'There's no point in having a go at Fred Clark's flimsy breadth of knowledge even though it's quite a tempting target. We'll only end up looking like bullies and he'll garner even more sympathy from the voters if we push him too hard. Nadine says that people won't really care if he knows diddly squat about local priorities. But no worries, folks - she's come up with an alternative way to bring down the golden boy .. and it's a cracker. Mind you, she had to shell out a fair bit of cash to tease out the info from his social circle because this guy is so well liked. Even so - as the saying goes - everyone has a price.'

Chief Tory spear carrier, Lesley Ashurst, shuffled uneasily in her chair when she sensed that dirty tricks were afoot; she had developed a secret crush on Fred, irrespective of his recently announced Lib Dem leanings, and couldn't help sounding quite downbeat when enquiring,

'What have you got on him, Ric? Nothing really too damaging I hope?'

'Come on, Les, surely the more damage we inflict the better it will be. Actually, it's a real humdinger - turns out that our little Sir Galahad has been putting it about a bit on his travels. We already know that he fathered a bus load of kids in tandem with Karen Craig and now we've got hold of cast iron proof that there could be loads more little bleeders carrying his DNA.'

Ric realised that most his associates were almost salivating in readiness for his revelations and he paused to build the excitement before ploughing on,

'All that working away from home offered Fred plenty of opportunities to cheat on his partner, and it looks like he got stuck in, er so to speak. Nadine took a trip up north to a haulage firm he used to work for and - thanks to her charming ways and my bank account - she managed to get a couple of his old flames to spill the beans. It looks like we've got enough material to go live with a cracking *love rat* smear story.'

There was a general rumble of satisfaction in the room but Ric noticed that Lesley's reaction was not exactly what he had anticipated when she commented,

'I'm not surprised about the women being reluctant to dob him in - after all, he's a bit of a hunk isn't he?'

'Who the hell cares about that? Get a bloody grip, Lesley! Anyway, I've sent all the lurid details to the local press and they can go to town on it. Nadine's guys will be bashing out a few leaflets as well and circulating them around the doors. I expect our man of the moment will not be so popular when respectable residents find out that he's been playing away. Oh, I can see the headlines now - *Captain Underpants Caught with his Trousers Down!!* - that has a nice ring doesn't it?'

The first time Rob heard about the scandalous Fred Clark revelations was when he read about them online. The editors of both the Gazette and Examiner had given up pestering him for newsworthy items during *Purdah* (Al Miron moaned that it would be easier to *get blood out of an effin' stone*) and Rob had been frozen out of their gossip loop temporarily.

The Gazette tried to achieve some impartiality in their piece about Fred's affairs by obtaining a quote from Karen Craig, which indicated that she and Fred enjoyed a very open relationship and had both indulged in the occasional dalliance with other sexual partners during their time together. Rob surmised that only a few liberal-minded readers would sympathise with such freewheeling views, and suspected that her remarks might do more harm than good. After all, she was actually admitting that she and her common law husband were well practised in the art of being unfaithful to each other and hence - in the eyes of many observers - untrustworthy.

He had no doubt that Jim Harvey would be gnashing his teeth and tearing out his thinning hair when he caught sight of the unwanted headlines about his erstwhile sure-fire candidate. Yet again, Rob was struck by the stunning ruthlessness of the Tory election apparatus. On a personal level, he felt sorry for Fred who seemed like a decent bloke, but local politics was a nasty business when *The Shark* and his retinue were up to their tricks.

Rob was thankful that he couldn't assist the press with enquiries about Fred's romantic liaisons, and he switched his attention to a more pressing personal matter - Sandy's request to visit his home and meet his mother. He had apparently passed muster with Mrs Staveley after her initial Caledonian grilling session, and his girlfriend was now keen to reciprocate so that she could make the acquaintance of Mrs Cummings and win her over. He was musing on the best way to introduce Sandy into his household when the phone rang and Lena Montgomery came on the line asking him for a comment about the latest scandal.

Rob was confused because he had already explained the intricacies of *Purdah* to the Gazette staff in great detail and he thought that the message had stuck, especially with Lena,

'Look, you know I can't give you a statement about a candidate's love life. I can ony recommend that you speak directly with the ,,'

Lena jumped in to stem his flow,

'No no Rob! You've got hold of the wrong end of the stick. I'm ringing about the other scandal. Surely you've seen the post about WDC on social media this morning?'

Normally Ozzie did a quick scan of one or two sites of note to track down references to the Council, but he was winding down prior to leaving Reilly Road and had taken annual leave for a couple of days to prepare for his new job. In the circumstances, Rob had to confess to Lena that he'd missed out on the latest news.

'Well, I suggest you look at Twitter as soon as you can. One of the contributors is querying the money spent on the WDC staff development scheme so I thought you might want to prepare a factual statement if you feel the need to correct any apparent misunderstandings. But you'd better hurry, Rob. It looks like this is going viral and I've been told to get something up on our website before I miss the boat and bigger fish begin to take the bait.'

Rob rang off and consulted the Twitter feeds that were usually reviewed every morning by Ozzie. And there it was as soon as he started browsing - a brief message posted by someone who was presumably a former WDC officer (hidden behind the cover name of *Truth Seeker*) alleging that the Council was wasting taxpayers' money on frivolous entertainments:

Believe it or not, while senior management at Reilly Road are telling us that they have to cut our services to the bone, they've still managed to find enough money to lay on a cabaret show for the staff. They say it's good for staff development - go figure!

To his dismay, the message was being retweeted rapidly and he was just about to shoot across to the Chief Exec's office to alert her when his phone buzzed again,

'Good morning, Woldwater District Council Press Office. Can I help? Oh hi Tom. Yes I know, I've just seen it. Oh, I agree it's making a bit of an impact on social media....no, of course it's not true - look, just give me half an hour and I'll get a statement sorted out.. no, I can assure you that I haven't given anything to Lena yet. No - I didn't know that she's posted a news item on the Gazette web page already. She told me she would hold off. Well, I can promise you that.. '

Rob was suddenly aware that Tom Irwin had hung up, no doubt to play catch up on the story. This prompted him to bring up the Gazette's news page on his monitor and he broke into a cold sweat when he took in the scurrilous article that Lena had concocted on the back of *Truth Seeker's* tweet. After printing a copy of Lena's poisonous prose - another task that would normally fall to Ozzie -

he made ready to scuttle off to Viv Bushby when his phone rang again. This time, a national daily was asking for the Press Office to comment on the *Future Journey* programme. Rob killed the call immediately, and then diverted further incoming messages to his voicemail.

His ex-wife Maria was in the outer office of the Chief Exec's suite when he barged through the door like his backside was on fire. To her surprise, Rob didn't find time for the usual pleasantries that they indulged in when he visited her workspace,

'Maria, love, I'm in a tearing hurry and I need a quick chat with Viv right now because we've gone viral. Can you arrange for me to see her straight away? I know she's busy but I have to see her.'

Chapter XXVII

Platters clatter calamitously

When Rob entered Viv's office suite a short while later, she was in the middle of a video conference call with Jim Harvey who was still spitting blood about his prize candidate being nobbled in East Woldchester. She looked up quizzically at the beleaguered comms officer and sighed,

'Is this really necessary, Rob? I'm knee deep in stuff with Cllr Harvey here - and Maria says you've caught a virus so I'm guessing that you shouldn't even be at work!'

'Eh? No, I'm fine thanks Viv. What I actually told Maria is that we've gone viral on social media. There's an incredibly iffy news story about our staff development scheme and we need to knock it on the head right away.'

'You know, I'm beginning to think you have gone down with something infectious, Rob. The *Future Journey* stuff is never really going to be mainstream news is it? I think you're overreacting, my lad, and I'm really busy right now.'

'Trust me Viv, I'm definitely not poorly. At least I thought I was feeling okay until I read what the Gazette is saying about us. You should have a look at the printout of their article right now and tell me what you want us to do. The national papers have also hitched on to this wagon and I've switched my calls to a recorded message. Heaven knows what will be piling up for me when I get back.'

'OK, Rob, hand it over and let's see what you're wittering on about.'

Viv scanned the item and her facial features tightened as she absorbed the content. Jim remained in contact via the video screen and was clearly irritated that his discussion with the Chief Exec had been railroaded by Rob's interruption. However, when she finished reading, the Leader could sense that she was perplexed. When he asked Viv if she was okay, she replied,

'Oh for goodness sake! What the hell is this load of crap? Jim, just listen to the opening paragraph.'

Is this a new low for Woldwater District Council? Bosses at the cash-strapped local authority recently gave £15,000 to a cabaret artist who cheered up the staff with his plate spinning skills while they prepared to undertake a so-called 'Future Journey'. Some observers

have suggested that the same performer should restore some balance to the authority's finances and reduce our Council tax bills.

Jim went ballistic,

'Bloody hell. What possessed her to spout this manure? The media love stories about councils acting like idiots, but surely Lena must know that this isn't true? Did we get any prior warning that the Gazette was going to publish this tosh?'

Rob piped up,

'No, not exactly. Lena rang a few weeks ago and asked Ozzie for information about Roger's programme so they could write an article about it for their business news. We sent them the overview package that we prepared for the staff and the press never covered it because, I suppose, they thought it was too boring.'

Jim was still incredulous,

'So how come they're coming up with all this nonsense about plate spinning?'

Rob sidestepped the question and said,

'An anonymous person - probably a staff member due to be laid off - posted a tweet about it and then Lena thought it was fair game.'

Before Jim could comment, Viv added,

'It looks like she's dug out extracts from the information pack that Ozzie sent her and she's taken them out of context to make us sound like imbeciles. It also doesn't really help our case when you see our quoted reference about needing to *improve our efficiency by encouraging the staff to adopt more agile mindsets, enabling them to assimilate future life lessons through immersion in ground-breaking learning techniques.* Who the hell said that?'

Rob plucked up the courage to reply,

'Actually that was attributed to Roger Pitt. It's taken from a joint memo from him and Jim that went out to all the WDC Heads of Service just before we announced that there would be a selective redundancy programme.'

Jim was rather flustered about being dragged into the mess, and cut in,

'Hey, I don't remember that form of words – that bloody chancer has been using my name in vain.'

Viv was reluctant to remind Jim that he had signed off on the text when Roger had wafted it in front of him. She motioned to Rob to stay quiet and then advised the Leader that, although Roger might have gone a bit OTT on the blurb, he had nevertheless achieved great success in introducing change programmes at a host of FTSE blue chip companies.

Jim was still on his high horse and wasn't receptive to any mollifying blandishments,

'That's all well and good, But, for the umpteenth time, what's all this nonsense about a plate spinner? Where on earth does all that come from?'

Again, Viv pre-empted Rob and replied,

'Roger gives inspiring motivational talks about new ways of working and then he finishes with a little bit of a flurry to embed his learning points in an entertaining way.'

Jim was on the brink of losing his cool,

'You mean he actually does some kind of soddin' cabaret act?

VIv was on the defensive and in danger of going down for the count,

'Er. Sort of I guess. He attaches plates to poles and gets people to start spinning them when he concludes his talk. He explains that the plate spinning represents all the tasks we have to deal with and he adds more to show how we can perform more efficiently through better teamwork. He does something similar with rings. It's all meant to show how two councils can unite and form an effective collaborative partnership. It goes down really well, Jim.'

'Obviously not with everyone! Especially if they're going to be laid off.'

Viv changed tack,

'We know that loads of councils are bringing in efficiency programmes to cut costs, and we should be pleased that we managed to nab Roger Pitt to direct our efforts. He's one of the best in the business when it comes to achieving workplace transformation. And don't forget that we engaged him at a knock down price because he fancied the challenge. He just does the plate stuff to liven up his presentations – and, personally, I don't see anything wrong with that.'

Jim wasn't convinced by any means,

'If just one single member of the staff takes exception that's all the media needs to get a daft story going. And technically they're not wrong about the entertainment. The press guys don't really care whether Roger is a good bloke and can motivate people. This cabaret story is a gimme for them - especially the fifteen grand price tag.'

Viv remained defiant,

'Well that's wrong anyway – it's only twelve grand. And that's the cost of the total package – you know, bespoke development modules for all our staff, change surgeries, motivational presentations. We'll save well over £200,000 in the end. Roger says that it's a fantastic *spend to save* measure. And don't forget that the full Council meeting approved the expenditure for Roger's programme. We're all in this together."

Jim sighed heavily, '

'Yes I get that. But if someone says that all we're getting for fifteen grand is a floor show you can see that it's a sitting duck - a turkey on a plate for some of the reptiles out there. Now then, dearest Rob, can we just talk to the paper and ask them to tone things down a bit?'

Rob explained that he would do his best but he couldn't guarantee a good outcome,

`Accuracy isn't exactly Lena's strong point so I'll see if I can get her to amend the story and frame it in a less sensational context. But I've a feeling that this whole thing might have gone too far now, especially with the nationals banging on our door.'

VIv was still hopeful,

'See what you can do about getting the Examiner to climb down, Rob, and then we'll take it from there. I tell you what - maybe we could ask Lena to come and sit in on a *Future Journey* staff workshop session to see what's really involved?'

Rob wasn't convinced,

'I think that ship has sailed. Might do more harm than good now.'

'OK then, Rob just make contact with the Gazette - and the Examiner - and see if they'll listen to reason. And I want you to come up with an official statement that I can smarten up and send to the world and his wife as soon as possible.'

Chapter XXVIII

Spinning again

Half an hour later Rob was back in Viv's domain to review a press statement that he'd prepared. Jim was still on the videolink and it was clear that he and the Chief Executive had been engaged in a heated discussion about the developing news story. Rob caught a distinct whiff of an acrimonious blame game that had been played out during his absence. They were certainly less than cordial to each other when Viv informed Jim tersely that Rob had returned and was going to read out his draft.

The nervous comms officer found it hard to remain impassive in such a frosty atmosphere and began rather hesitantly ,

'Er, this is like er what I have so far..

Woldwater District Council prides itself on its highly skilled and knowledgeable staff and is always looking for ways to develop their expertise further.

Despite severe cutbacks in central government funding over the last few years, we have maintained a good level of customer satisfaction with the services we provide thanks to a wide range of initiatives we have introduced, including a very successful efficiency programme and the introduction of some work sharing with another local authority.

Jim interrupted Rob while he was in full flow,

'Can we get rid of the term *severe* when we're talking about cuts to central government funding? Believe it or not, we got off quite lightly compared with some authorities and I wouldn't want to risk a rocket from the local MP and a complete nuking of our budget by the Tories next time around.'

Rob continued reading out the statement,

We are now preparing for a deepening of our links with West Fordham District Council, which will widen our pool of expertise and resources and also allow us to benefit from wider economies of scale. This has already enabled us to make a modest reduction in staff numbers through a selective redundancy scheme.

He broke off with a query,

'I haven't mentioned the likelihood of even more job cuts in the future – do you think we should?'

Jim vociferously opposed going down that route,

'No way Jose! Leave that to one side for the time being. The *economies of scale* stuff is a bit nerdy, though. How about just saying: *allow us to achieve better value for money.*

Rob agreed that Jim's suggestion was more in keeping with the Council's mantra,

'Fine by me – we'll have to prepare some frequently asked questions to go along with the statement, but the *value for money* tag is always good for gravitas. Now here's the really important bit,

To ensure we make the most of these emerging partnerships, we have embarked on the Future Journey staff development programme. This will help our officers adjust to new ways of working by providing them with unique opportunities to cut across traditional boundaries, with the assistance of an advanced toolkit which explores new career development avenues.

Vlv intervened,

'That's exactly what we should be stressing. The wording's a bit out there but it's on the right lines.'

Rob confessed,

'I nicked it from the text in Roger Pitt's company prospectus. Here's some more of his blurb that we can use,

The development programme has been created by the award-winning workplace transformation expert Roger Pitt and provides staff with personalised training modules to identify their favoured learning styles. The programme also includes bespoke group exercises and interventions to prepare employees for enhanced partnership working.

Jim was slightly apprehensive,

'We're getting a bit nerdy again – but I think we can just about live with it if we need to get this out quickly.'

Rob then readied himself to deliver his coup de grace,

'Here's the clincher,

The cost of the whole scheme equates to about £3 per employee and it is expected that it will generate savings of over £200,000 within the next eighteen months.

This time Jim was more impressed,

'That's quite neat, Rob. It's not even the price of a pint per person is it? But what about the cabaret stuff? Shouldn't we say something? After all, this is what we're getting slagged off about.'

Rob anticipated his query,

'Well, that's all wrapped up in the stuff about *bespoke group exercises and interventions* and I think we should leave it buried in there if we can. If we're put on the spot by the media, we should just front up and give them the spiel about plate spinning skills demonstrating the need for new ways of working – and then leave it at that.'

Vlv was cautiously optimistic,

'Yes - I think that might actually work. Well done, Rob. Let's hope this puts all this nonsense to bed eh? Maybe we can talk to the local BBC bods and arrange an official interview to hammer home where we are coming from on this.'

Jim agreed that going on the front foot was a good idea,

'You seem to have a good grasp of the basics on this one, Rob. You can check with Meera but I think that the *Purdah* restrictions don't apply to this issue as we've got sufficient reason to step up and address a serious misunderstanding about the Council. Hey, perhaps you should do the interview. We could ask for Anita Vernon to do the honours - she's my favourite.'

Rob tried to keep a straight face but he was screaming inside. He was being asked to appear on TV and act as the fall guy in the midst of a public shellacking.

Chapter XXIX

While the prat's away..

At the same time as Rob was quaking in his boots about his forthcoming trial by television, Nadine Hurley was getting ready for a more pleasurable sort of earth moving event. To be precise, she was preparing the ground for a romantic liaison at her Woldshire base - the swanky lakeside home that she shared with Ric. She congratulated herself yet again on having persuaded *The Shark* to purchase the property and was well chuffed with the alterations she had commissioned to add a substantial *oomph* effect. It was a huge relief to see the back of the builders after twelve long weeks of hammering and drilling and - now that the dust had settled - Nadine felt the time was right for the sort of banging that she preferred!

Ric had gone off to campaign around the disgraced Cllr Horsfield' South Titbury stamping ground and Nadine had invited Wayne Kerr, the Tory candidate for the ward, to come over so they could review his stellar progress and plan his next moves. When he arrived, it didn't take long for her and Wayne to reassure themselves that all the feedback from doorsteps showed he was heading for a landslide victory. Instead of discussing further tactics, Nadine suggested that they should rest on their laurels and open a bottle of champagne to celebrate his forthcoming success. She ushered him into the newly completed conservatory and indicated that he might like to sit on the rattan sofa while she sought the wine and her partner's finest crystal goblets.

Having been a bit of a philanderer in the past, Wayne understood what was going on from the outset, and he wasn't surprised in the least when Nadine reappeared clad only in a loosely tied silk kimono and bearing gifts of fizz and nibbles. She told him to make room for her on the sofa and squeezed against his toned body. Although he was now married with two kids, Wayne liked to think that he might still be an active player in the casual sex stakes when the opportunity presented itself. He wasn't going to turn down the chance of becoming much better acquainted with the power behind the Sharkey throne, but it struck him that she was making all the moves and - to his amazement - he felt slightly coy in her presence.

Nevertheless, as soon as the Bollinger was drained like it was going out of fashion, any lingering inhibitions on the part of Wayne were shed and he disrobed quickly as he contemplated fornication with the femme fatale who was waiting patiently for him to play catch up. Nadine often loved foreplay better than sex and, when she was nibbling Wayne's ear, she hit him with a killer line that had come to her earlier that day,

'Wayne dear, I've really been looking forward to forging a closer relationship with the future member for South Titbury - and, from what I can see it looks like a very nice member indeed!'

Wayne guffawed, and tried to reciprocate with a witty remark of his own,

'I'm glad it meets with your approval, m'lady - and as I'm moving into the world of politics soon, I guess you could say that it's a Right Honourable Upstanding Member!'

Nadine giggled and was satisfyingly merry as the wine kicked in. She was anticipating a cheeky little romp with a very tasty geezer for an hour or so, and everything was going to plan. Just as she was about to wriggle out of her kimono, her romantic idyll was halted in its tracks when she reacted to what sounded like a large SUV approaching on the gravel driveway.

'Oh shit. I think that might be Ric. Why the hell is he back so early?'

Nadine handed Wayne his pile of abandoned clothes and told him to sort himself out while she ran into the master bedroom and retrieved the garments that she had been wearing when her partner left earlier that morning. Luck was on their side and they both managed to get dressed before *The Shark* was unlocking the front door . At the last minute, Nadine spied a packet of condoms on the coffee table and she motioned to Wayne to pocket it just before Ric made his grand entrance.

He strode into the conservatory and was delighted to see them both huddled over a sheaf of ridiculously anal spreadsheets that he'd compiled to analyse voter intentions in South Titbury. But when he spotted an empty champagne bottle on the coffee table, he switched to serious mode,

'That's a bit premature isn't it? It's not a done deal until election day, you know.'

'Don't be a party pooper, RIc. Wayne's as good as over the line now. Anyway, I thought you said that you were going off to do a spot of canvassing in Titbury to seal the deal once and for all?'

'Well, yes - and it was going well. Just as you suggested, I was hanging around the local supermarket to fly the flag for Wayne, and I bumped into this bloke who started moaning about WDC being full of perverts. Apparently, he recently drove his wife and kid into Woldchester and he says that he left them inside the car for a while because he needed to buy some groceries. He reckons that a traffic warden came across to the car, took a photo of the kid in the back seat, and then issued a fine for exceeding the time limit for parking.'

Nadine feigned interest and tried to chivvy him along,

'Why how interesting, darling. But why the rush to get back here? Surely, you should still be out there winning hearts and minds.'

Ric moved on to his grand reveal,

' I know where you're coming from, darling - but this story gets better if you just listen. Anyway, the bloke complained to the Council about the photo and they grudgingly let him off the penalty. But the Legal Advisor practically told him to sod off when he made allegations about paedophiles and they wouldn't give him the time of day. So he goes to the local press with his tale of woe and they ignore him as well. That's all a bit rum isn't it? He's in my car now - I've invited him over to get some more details for my podcast because I reckon there's another killer smear story in there somewhere.'

Nadine was royally huffed about missing her afternoon delight with a lithe young beefcake and commented starchily,

'You'll have to watch your step if you keep on gunning for the WDC officers, Ric. There's an excellent chance that you'll soon be the

203

Leader at Reilly Road and they'll remember how much you pissed them off on your way up.'

RIc wasn't buying her reprimanding tone,

'They're all pathetic losers and I'm doing no harm keeping them on their toes. Wait until I get Joe Baxter on board with his *Dyno Active* performance monitoring system - you'll really see the fur fly then.'

Wayne interrupted their icy exchange,

'Er, I can see that you're both going to be busy. I'll let myself out shall I?'

Reluctantly Nadine nodded her assent and steeled herself to be pleasant to yet another waif and stray with a grudge against the Council. At times like these, she longed to be back in her London apartment away from distractions to her libido.

Chapter XXX

Trial by TV

Rob retired wearily to the pub around the corner from the Council offices at the end of an exhausting day and joined Ozzie and his mates for a consoling pint after dealing with the fall out from the troublesome cabaret story. Ozzie had a head start on him at the bar and he and his cronies were already on their second round of drinks.

Ozzie's mate Gibbo was the first to see Rob enter and yelled,

'Hey guys, it's Rob the juggling expert from the Council - so it must be time for some serious clubbing! Get it?'

Rob glared at him and spat out his retort,

'It's not juggling, cloth ears - it's plate spinning. Just like my bloody head is doing at the moment.'

Ozzie was counting down the days prior to departing from the Council and he was still in a buoyant mood in contrast to Rob's dismal fug. He'd returned from leave early to assist in the office when Rob issued a cry for help to deal with the extra tasks arising from *Plate Gate*. Unlike his deflated superior, he was buzzing because an event at WDC was such hot news,

'It's been full on, that's for sure. I think we might even merit extra coverage tomorrow. Exciting or what?'

Rob took a sip of his IPA and moaned,

'Exciting? It's been a piggin' awful day! I honestly didn't think that phone could ring so much without packing up. I'm absolutely knackered fobbing off so many callers with our flaky official statement.'

Ozzie chipped in,

'I'm pretty whacked too, boss. Don't forget all my online monitoring today. I still can't figure why everyone is so bothered about a few plates spinning, for God's sake. There's wars going on, post-Covid poverty, Royal spats, food banks and Brexit buyer's remorse to be going on with.'

Rob explained,

'That's why all the reporters are constantly searching for a bit of light relief. Everyone loves to read all that stuff about taxpayer's money going down the drain, and it's even better when Council workers look like prize dicks into the bargain.'

Another dimwit in Ozzie's circle chipped in,

'Well you lot do live the life of Reilly Road, eh? Anyway, as far as entertainment goes I reckon it would be much better for your entertainer chappie to keep a few beers on the go at the same time, ha? Hey, maybe we can do that tonight - and just for Rob, we'll order some plates of food so we can all spin them after we've eaten?'

Rob didn't join in with the banter,

'Why can't we just talk about football as usual? There's a big match on TV tonight ... let's see if they've switched the pub telly to the right channel. Oh bollocks - that's all I needed, the regional news is on the screen now. They'll be running that toe curling interview I recorded this afternoon with the bolshy BBC reporter. I told Viv and Jim it was a bad idea but they insisted. I've been trying to avoid the damn thing on the afternoon news bulletins, and I thought the pub would be a safe haven.'

Ozzie looked a little sheepish and confessed,

'Hope you don't mind, Rob, but I asked the bar staff to tune in – we don't really want to miss your tete a tete with the gorgeous Anita Vernon do we?'

At that moment, Rob would have gladly ripped the head off his young colleague and fed it into the anaerobic digester at the Council's bio waste plant. He attempted a menacing scowl but Ozzie had looked away by then and he and his mates were glued to the TV as the presenter introduced the item,

'As the row about unnecessary spending of taxpayers money escalates, Anita Vernon spoke to Woldwater District Council spokesman Rob Cummings and here is what he had to say on the matter.'

Ozzie became extremely animated and could hardly contain himself,

'Here it comes..ssh everybody!'

The camera panned to Rob, standing to attention on the steps of Reilly Road in his best suit, and trying to stick rigidly to his flimsy official brief,

'The cost of the entire Future Journey scheme works out at £3 for each participant, and we expect to see savings of over £200,000 over the next eighteen months or so. That's extremely good value.'

'And how can you be so sure about those savings, Mr Cummings?'

'So the brains behind the development programme, er Roger Pitt, has an enviable track record, and all the FTSE 100 organisations he

has worked with in the past have been able to make big reductions in running costs thanks to his unique user-friendly techniques.'

'Such as Ye Olde Worlde Gourmet Cakes company for instance? If I'm not mistaken, they sacked seventy people after he advised them on improving their performance. In fact the dismissals were so efficiently carried out that the redundancy notices were conveyed to the workers by text message.'

'Sorry, I have no idea about the Old er Cakes business model and....'

'But you did bring up the fact that Mr. Pitt has had dealings with a range of companies. So using Olde Worlde Gourmet as a past precedent, can you comment on the job prospects for employees at your Council? We know that you've already laid some staff off.'

'So let's be clear, Woldwater District Council is a great place to work and offers fantastic career opportunities going forward, especially now that we have the Future Journey staff development programme up and running.'

'But can you confirm that there will be no further job losses?'

'So, like most local authorities, we have introduced a selective redundancy programme which applies to a very small proportion of staff - and we are working with them all to ensure that they are well prepared to seek equivalent work elsewhere.'

'I believe that two of those affected are Pest Control Officers. Does this mean your Council won't be providing that particular customer service as part of your Future Journey?'

*'So, erm retaining officers with that specialty on a long term
contract basis wasn't cost effective going forward. In fact, we
discovered that residents could get a better deal in terms of that
particular service on the open market.'*

*'It still seems odd that you're letting that sort of skilled person go
and yet your organisation has funds to run a cabaret style
entertainment show.'*

'So, Anita,can I just correct a misunderstanding about...'

*'That's all we have time for. Thank you Mr Cummings - and now
back to the studio.'*

Watching the horror show unfold, Rob was equally as livid as he had
been when the cameras had stopped rolling earlier in the day and
he'd given Anita an Anglo Saxon rollicking.

Ollie didn't do subtlety very well and observed,

'Well I guess that it could have been worse - possibly? And why did
you start so many sentences with *So*? It grates a bit if I'm being
honest.'

'Oh, I don't know - must have rubbed off on me when I was
listening to that crap artist Joe Baxter and his ramblings about the
Dyno Interactive cutting edge mullarkey. This is all just a nightmare.
I wish we'd never gone anywhere near Roger Pitt and his ridiculous
journey. We'll just have to hunker down and wait until people get
fed up with our sideshow and move on to fresh barmy allegations
that some other poor sap will have to fend off. Maybe the Gods will
deliver a Government leadership meltdown again, or a B *List*

celebrity might be waiting in the wings to smash up a chip shop or perhaps go on a bonking spree...oh, that's been done with Fred Clark hasn't it?'

'You're right, though, Rob. There's always a daft news story breaking somewhere, and my old Dad used to say that today's headlines are tomorrow's chip papers. Not sure what he meant by that but I think I got the drift.'

Rob was about to explain to the callow novice that takeaway fish suppers used to be wrapped in newspaper when he glimpsed Ric Sharkey and his Tory goon squad working their way into the snug at the back of the pub.

Before Rob could take evasive action, the much reviled councillor spotted him and diverted into the bar with his entourage trailing behind him,

'Ah, our official spokesman! Caught the interview before we convened our Shadow Cabinet meeting this afternoon. I must say that you couldn't have done more to look the part, Rob, but it's a pity about the paper-thin excuses that you had to trot out when you were defending the slurs about the cabaret act.'

Rob's hackles rose and he countered,

'I didn't hear you or your colleagues dissenting about the *Future Journey* programme when the Chief Exec briefed the full Council about it a few months ago.'

'Ah, well I think you've got a selective memory, young Mr Cummings. I admit that I didn't vote against the initiative, but I did abstain after saying that there were better ways to save money. I've also mentioned my party's uneasiness about Roger Pitt a few times in my newsletters to residents. We've looked into alternatives, you see, and it's my firm belief that Joe Baxter should get the green light to introduce his *Dyno Active* scheme if we want to make sensible savings. And, what's more, he can't do cabaret acts to save his life, so it would spare us all from a spot of unnecessary embarrassment.'

Having made his point, amid a flurry of titters from his sycophants, *The Shark* flounced off towards the lounge to celebrate the impressive Tory lead in the local opinion polls.

Rob perked up a bit after his adrenalin-boosting joust with Sharkey and the positive trajectory of events increased when Ozzie nudged him and said ,

'Oh, wow, Mr Popular, here comes your school teacher friend, and it looks like she's not marking any homework tonight.'

Rob had texted Sandy to tell her that he was drowning his sorrows and he was genuinely touched that she had made the effort to drop everything and seek him out. But he was baffled when she was so cheery,

'Hi Robster Lobster. What's it like to be so famous then?'

'Sand,I really don't know what you mean...'

'Well, it's not every day that you're on the TV news is it? I reckon it must be rather exhilarating.'

'Look, love – no offence but I've been getting an absolute battering in public today, and I looked like a prize cabbage into the bargain. It's a miserable experience, believe me.'

'Come on, Rob. It still means you're getting noticed doesn't it? You've become a bit of an instant celeb in my Mum's group of friends. And, if you're lucky, your quirky little story could go national. It's already on YouTube and they've spliced up your comments to fit with the tune of *You spin me round*. My Mum can't stop going on about you and she's humming the ditty all the time. It's really cool!'

'Hang on a minute. Are you actually saying that you think this ridiculous mess is a good thing?'

'Well it is kinda silly more than anything else isn't it? Just a bit of a laugh really. Anyway, seeing as you're wearing your best suit, how about going out for another meal tonight? Perhaps we can talk more about your interview somewhere more intimate than this grotty bar? You know, people don't really pay much attention to the actual content of the news so there's no need to get so spun up - oh dear, I'm sorry. Freudian slip eh? Anyway, you can tell me all about Anita Vernon. My Mum loves the outfits she wears.'

'I er suppose we could eat out tonight. In fact, I haven't even had any lunch today. I thought I'd lost my appetite completely but I can probably find room for a decent lasagne and a nice drop of Montepulciano. Yeah – let's go for it, Sand.'

Ozzie was clearly disappointed that Rob would not be sitting in a sulk for the rest of the evening, and pleaded,

'Hey, aren't you going to stay and finish your pint, Rob?'

'Good shout, Ozzie. Oh, and here's a new cabaret highlight for you - the disappearing act!

He downed his beer in one long gulp and then rose from his chair to escort Sandy out of the bar. As he departed with his girlfriend on his arm, he bid a bullish farewell to the lads,

'You know, today might not be as bad as I expected after all – see you later, losers.'

Chapter XXXI

Famous for five minutes .. or so

Just as Sandy predicted, Rob was beginning to realise that many people didn't take in much of the content when local news bulletins were aired, and were much more focused on spotting people or places they knew. For that reason, Ada Cummings was thrilled that her son had featured in the headline spot. Sandy was on her inaugural visit to the house that Ada and Rob shared, and the BBC interview served as a wonderful ice breaker for the women, even though Rob was desperate to change the subject.

It was clear that his Mum had never had so much attention paid to her for years, and she was milking her moment in the sun,

'Even this crotchety bloke in the greengrocers said that he'd seen Rob on the news, Sandy. He never speaks normally but I asked him for a pound of plums and he popped in an extra one for my *famous son*!'

Sandy was just as bubbly when discussing the issue,

'I know, it was great in the restaurant last night. We got a fantastic table and they gave us a free round of drinks! The waiter even asked for Rob's autograph. It's like Andy Warhol predicted - Rob is having his fifteen minutes of fame.'

Ada was a bit bamboozled,

'I don't know him, lass. Andy Warhorse? Does he live around here?'

Rob interjected,

'No Mum, he's dead. Anyway, my fifteen minutes of whatsit should be up now I reckon. Now how about we focus on what's for tea?'

Ada wasn't going to be pushed off course while she was indulging in a rare bout of vicarious stardom. Since her husband had kicked the bucket, her life had not been a bed of roses, and she wasn't used to being the centre of attention in her social circle,

'Oh I'm making a cottage pie, Rob. Now as I was saying to Sandy, the WI women have been on to me about Rob's TV appearance and they want him to do a talk for them on media handling - you'll do it, son, won't you?'

'Yes Mum. Anything for a quiet life.'

Sandy was amused by the exchanges between mother and son and clearly felt comfortable in contrast to Rob's awkwardness when he first encountered her Mum and underwent such a rigorous interrogation.Ordinarily, Sandy would have been subjected to a similar barrage of questions, but Rob's trial by TV was the topic *du jour* and everything else was off the agenda. His mother was obviously very proud of him, and Sandy guessed that he didn't mind her cheery gossip half as much as he claimed.

Ada and Sandy disappeared into the kitchen to sort out the dinner but he could still hear them prattling about the interview as they worked in tandem.

'The man down the road thinks that it will be on that funny TV show about the news events of the week. Imagine my Rob on that?'

'Oh, I think that's a shoo-in, Ada. My Mum says he looked very distinguished and gave a good account of himself. That's high praise coming from her..'

'Rob says that it's not a cabaret show really. The man just does a little trick at the end of an ordinary pep talk.'

'Yes, that's what he told me as well, and he says the staff workshop sessions trundle along a bit and aren't very interesting. But you can see why the news people love this story can't you?'

Rob tried to blot out the inane chatter in the background, and turned his attention to the emails on his work phone. He hadn't had time to check his in-box during the mayhem arising from *Plate Gate* and he began to catch up with them at a steady pace.

As he was ploughing through a tsunami of messages, one of the more recent ones made him sit up and take special notice. The *Future Journey* architect Roger Pitt had contacted the Chief Exec (with a copy to Rob) seeking an urgent meeting the next day to try and head off the harsh criticism that they had both been receiving. Roger wrote that he was desperate to *get Plate Gate off the top of the whacky charts* and would be brainstorming suggestions to tamp things down. A response from Vlv Bushby agreed to the initiative and she directed Rob to attend a video conference at ten o'clock the next morning.

Chapter XXXII

The calm after the media storm?

Rob rose from his bed the next day with a tiny flutter of hope in his breast, and he travelled to the office in a positive frame of mind. Ozzie had arrived well ahead of him and observed with a tinge of sadness that the national tabloids had moved on from baiting Roger Pitt and were now lambasting an heiress who had made a killing on the sale of dodgy Personal Protection Equipment during the Covid lockdown. One newspaper featured a silly rumour that Roger Pitt had been approached to do a slot on *Britain's Got Talent* but the man himself had declined to comment. There wasn't much else that the article could add, which explained why it had been relegated to a page near the rear end of the publication.

Ozzie also noticed that, while references to *Plate Gate* were still popping up sporadically in cyberspace, there were fewer related memes than the day before and the PPE scandal was successfully diverting a lot of attention away from the woes of Woldwater. Rob informed his junior colleague about the forthcoming video conference with Roger and Viv, and they both trusted that it might result in a spirited fight back against the barbs that had been directed non-stop against WDC.

216

Nevertheless, there was a significant grey cloud emerging on the local news horizon because Ozzie's media monitoring session had turned up Ric Sharkey's new video newsletter to residents, hammering the Council's track record on providing value for money, and promising radical changes as soon as he took over as Leader. Ozzie brought it up on his screen and he and Rob watched despondently as the *enfant terrible* of Reilly Road did his worst:

'It gives me no pleasure to stand here and criticise the budget proposals outlined by the Leader of the Council a few weeks ago, but I am compelled to voice my grave concerns.

'I cannot dispute that Woldshire District Council - in keeping with many other local authorities - is under enormous budgetary pressures, mostly due to the ongoing austerity measures that are absolutely necessary to steady the good ship United Kingdom. Having said that, I believe that this Council's proposals for the next financial year are totally inept. I was opposed to last year's budgetary recommendations - that were only approved by a wafer thin majority - because I knew that this is just not the right time to raise parking charges, cut back on the regularity of waste collections and increase our share of your Council Tax bill.

'Yes, times are hard, my friends, but there are other ways and means of reducing our costs without burdening the taxpayer so much. The current WDC staff development programme should be helping us reach that goal, but it has failed miserably and is now a laughing stock across the nation. Instead of upskilling our valued workers to achieve more with less, the current administration has been treating them to expensive cabaret shows, and maybe even other entertainments that haven't been disclosed yet.

'Mark my words, the Council's Leader, Jim Harvey, should be held to account for this fiasco - he is Woldwater's very own Emperor Nero, playing his fiddle while Rome is burning. And fiddling is the appropriate word to describe how the Lib Dems are operating - there seems to be a bit of a fiddle going on right now to deprive residents of the services that they deserve!

'So I'm urging everyone who has a say in the upcoming by-elections in South Titbury and East Woldchester to use your vote wisely and help the Conservatives take control of WDC so we can guarantee a better future for you and your families.'

Not for the first time, Rob admired the chutzpah of *The Shark* and his relentless vote winning tactics. The electioneering skills deployed by RIc, and the rest of his Tory brethren, were head and shoulders above the creaky efforts of their Lib Dem opponents and, the way things were panning out, both of the latter's by-election candidates were heading for a complete trouncing.

It was no surprise when the Tory tormentor popped his head around the door of Rob's office a few minutes later,

'Ah - I see the press team is hard at work as usual. I bet you've been rushed off your feet with all that *Plate Gate* stuff! Just wanted to make sure that you've seen my latest video and that you're up to date with the party's latest views. When I get to be the *Grand Fromage* around here that's going to be the way we communicate most of the time. Press releases are yesterday's thing and I'll be looking for someone who has excellent video editing skills rather than just a dusty old wordsmith, no offence Rob.'

'None taken, Cllr Sharkey. By the way, I hear that Roger Pitt is planning to set the record straight on the allegations about his development programme. Just so you know.'

'Good luck to him on that one. Now I have to toddle off because I'm chasing up Albert Suddick in Environmental Services about fly tipping. I've been asking him to let me know when the latest figures will be published as they should be due really soon - they're published by a third party so you can't hide them away under your local *Purdah* smokescreen, Rob. I hear that WDC's position in the performance charts might have nosedived, judging by the rumours doing the rounds. That will be another little mess for you to clean up in the Press Office, eh lads? Ooh, look I've just made a little joke and I didn't even realise it. I must be feeling quite chipper today. Seriously, though, we need to keep emphasising our zero tolerance policy on illegal waste dumping and I firmly believe that prosecutions for fly tippers should carry jail sentences - and you can quote me on that when I'm Leader.'

Ric then scurried off to the relief of Rob and Ozzie, who were sickened by his arrogant manner and veiled threats. Rob summed up his reaction to the latest visitation,

'That twerp will destroy this Council the way he's going around dissing us all of the time. He shouldn't be pestering any of our officers at the moment with the two by-elections on the go, but what's the point of telling him? Anyway, Albert can take care of himself and he's quite capable of telling Ric to sod off when he's not wanted.'

Ozzie opined that he was leaving Reilly Road at an opportune time, and expressed sympathy for those remaining. Rob agreed with him and summed up the dire situation,

'Do you know, Oz, I honestly think that *The Shark* will turn this place into an undermanned gig economy workhouse and then brag that he's some kind of financial Messiah when he doesn't increase WDC's portion of the Council Tax bill. I expect he'll have moved on to Westminster before people realise the damage that he's done, and I don't reckon he'll give a hamster's arse.'

Ozzie perceived a sharp downturn in Rob's mood after Ric's untimely intervention, and tried to resurrect the early morning wave of cheerfulness that they had surfed by turning his attention back to Roger Pitt,

'At least the *Future Journey* chap is good fun isn't he? And even though he's been getting some grief of late, you can't argue about him putting us on the map. Even my cousin Kieran in Edinburgh knows about WDC and the plate tricks. He works in a factory up there and he told me that his mates were all talking about it in the canteen when the kitchen staff were clearing up after lunch. He joked about bringing some sticks in to see if they could do a bit of spinning with the used plates but the manager told him that they would have to pay for the damaged crockery when it all went wrong. Of course, that wouldn't happen with Roger because he's ace isn't he?''

Rob took in what his colleague said and replied,,

'Well, I suppose that it would be a big embarrassment for Roger if the plates shattered all over the place. Hey, hang on a minute - I think you might have stumbled on something that could work in our favour. Oz, you and your cousin just might be the answer to our prayers!.'

Rob got his head down immediately and started to draft furiously, not pausing for his usual cup of tea and cake while he put together a suggestion to boost WDC's reputation. He then touched base with Viv Bushby and Roger Pitt at the video conference and it didn't last too long because they gleefully agreed to the proposal arising from his chance conversation with Ozzie.

Half an hour later Lena Montgomery of the Gazette was waiting patiently in the WDC reception area on the promise of what was described to her on the phone as an important follow-up to the staff development scheme saga.

When Rob came to collect her, he was grinning from ear to ear so she presumed that he was in a receptive mode - unlike the grumpy version of the same guy who had rudely told her to bugger off when she had previously requested fresh info about *Plate Gate*. He summoned her into a conference room and, when she was seated, he said,

'Thanks for coming over at short notice, Lena. I just wanted you to be the first to know that Roger Pitt is going to make a statement to counter the criticism that he's received. You can have a copy of his spiel in advance of anyone else if you agree to quote him word for word. If you play ball, we think that he - and WDC - can achieve some transparency in the matter and earn a bit of credit after all the damage you've done.'

Lena gritted her teeth when she was being criticised, and defended her corner like a tiger,

'Now, come on! That story was fair game when all's said and done, Rob. You can't expect me to ignore a scoop like that when it comes knocking at my door? I already had the Council's blurb about the scheme and included some of it in my original story if you didn't notice. I do have some integrity, you know."

Rob wasnt buying Lena's attempt to justify her actions,

'Yes, but you played fast and loose with our text and chopped it around to make us sound like imbeciles. Anyway, that's water under the bridge and I think it would be appropriate if the person who dropped us in this quagmire can help us find a way out.'

'Well you just can't tell me to publish Roger's statement in full and not even express my opinion.'

'Alright I'll take that response as a *No Deal*. You've had your chance and you've blown it. Now get lost and leave me in peace so I can talk to Tom at the Examiner - your loss will be his gain.'

'Oh, it's like that is it? Alright then, I promise I'll try to go easy on you guys if there's no justification for sticking the knife in again. Now please let me see what you've got?'

Rob handed over the statement that he'd finalised in consultation with Roger and Viv a short while earlier.

Lena studied it with care and reacted in the way that Rob had anticipated,

'Ooh. This is good stuff. Yes. I like it! You know, I reckon this will do very nicely, Rob.'

'I'm sure it will. Might even boost your chances of working on a national paper as well, eh?'

Chapter XXXIII

Roger dodges!

True to her word, Lena raced back to the Gazette office and convinced her editor to hold off printing the latest hard copy edition to make room for her scoop. She then dashed off a new front page article courtesy of Rob's statement, taking care to emphasise that it was an exclusive for the paper. Meanwhile, her boss scrapped his original editorial about a gas leak in Titbury and compiled a pithy item which dovetailed nicely with Lena's big news. When the paper finally hit the streets the next day, Lena clicked the button to upload the online version of her story, enabling her to enjoy two bites of the same cherry.

Within minutes, the online scoop was spreading across newsgroups, and Rob and Ozzie began coping with a renewed surge of interest in the activities of Roger Pitt - this time with a spring in their step as most queries were very positive and engaging. One of the first callers to their office was Anita Vernon from the BBC and, despite being roasted alive by her a few days earlier, Rob was the picture of politeness when he lined up an interview with Roger for her daily news bulletin.

The hard pressed pair broke off from their hectic pace of work at midday and sat back to watch the lunch time regional news slot on the Comms Office TV. Viv Bushby also attended the viewing with her fingers firmly crossed when the announcer appeared on the screen:

'News is breaking in the local press about a fresh twist to the plate spinner story at Woldwater District Council. Anita Vernon is with Roger Pitt, the renowned staff development specialist, to bring us up to date with the latest developments.'

Anita was perched on a large Chesterfield sofa in Roger's lavish London apartment and was all sweetness and light,

'Roger – I understand that you've struck a new deal with the Council following what you describe as unfair criticism of the methods you employ as part of your staff development module.'

Roger was equally serene and trilled,

'I have indeed Anita. After discussions with the Leader and the Chief Executive, I am so confident about the future success of the Future Journey scheme that I will not charge a single penny for my services until the authority has made the savings envisaged over the next eighteen months.'

'Let's get this right for clarity's sake. The Council will not pay any money to you if you cannot save them at least £200,000 in running costs?'

'That's correct, Anita. It may seem too good to be true but I am angry that my reputation has been maligned and I want to set the

record straight by making this gesture. That is why I'm willing to forgo my fees if I don't succeed - or, if you will, send the spinning plates crashing to the floor.'

'And does that mean you won't be doing any more flamboyant demonstrations to illustrate learning points for the staff?'

'Well I've garnered lots of plaudits for my unique motivational methods but I suspect that there won't be any more - shall we say - "eye catching" diversions which the media might misconstrue. The basic point to stress, Anita, is that this is a genuine offer and the Council have informed me that they will be very pleased to accept it. Local residents can rest assured that if Woldwater DIstrict Council does have to pay out £12,000 for my development programme at the end of the day, it will mean that I have successfully delivered great value-for-money services while saving them a small fortune.'

He continued in spirited fashion,

'Being a taxpayer myself, I realise that councils must find new ways to reduce their running costs while looking after their most valuable resource – their employees . As you know well, Anita, there are some brutal ways of finding economies that don't exactly prioritise workers' rights. You've previously raised my association with the redundancies at Ye Olde Worlde Gourmet Cakes company.'

Anita perked up,

'Yes. It's shameful the way those people were treated.'

Roger was delighted that she took the bait and resumed,

'I totally agree. But most commentators seem to have missed that I intervened personally after the redundancies were announced and set up an assistance scheme which aimed to redeploy the workers who were laid off. I'm pleased to tell you that it paid off because almost sixty of the seventy people made redundant secured new jobs within weeks. And that's not all - quite a few of them are earning higher wages and enjoying better terms and conditions than they ever did at the cake factory.'

Anita looked rather cowed and glossed over her shoddy research,

'Erm, looking ahead, Roger, have you anything further to say to the folks in Woldwater District?'

'Only one thing really. In the extremely unlikely event of things not working out as planned at the Council, you will not be out of pocket. Now that's what I call a great balancing act. Hah!'

'Hah, yes, very good. Well, you heard it here live. Taxpayers really can't complain about Roger Pitt's incredibly generous offer.'

'Oh, and I almost forgot, Anita. Now that he doesn't have to pay me up front, the Leader of the Council Jim Harvey says he will restore the Memory Clubs for residents with dementia that were closed last year due to the cutbacks in spending.'

'Well, I agree that's extremely good news as well. And now back to the studio.'

The viewers in the WDC Comms Office were cockahoop because the interview had gone according to plan, and Viv was the first to comment,

'That was brilliant, lads! Maybe we can finally put the whole cabaret fiasco to bed now. How the hell can the public criticise us when a specialist is offering his services for free? You did a hell of a good job coming up with that idea, Rob.'

'Actually, Ozzie gave me the inspiration when he got me thinking about whether the *Future Journey* might not deliver what it said on the tin.'

'Oh, then very well done to you Ozzie! Alright then, I must be off - I'm due across at West Fordham for a full Council meeting this afternoon.'

When she left the room, Ozzie turned to Rob and said,

'Hey, thanks man. There was no need to big me up. I'm leaving in a short while and you were earning valuable brownie points there.'

Rob shrugged his shoulders and replied,

'Yes, but if things go wrong for you in the new job, you might need a glowing reference from Viv - er, provided she's still in post by then. I expect Ric will want to make a lot of changes when he takes over and I'm not sure that she'll be sticking around. Perhaps I'll be looking elsewhere as well.'

They returned to the main task of dealing with queries relating to Roger's statement, but it was already apparent that good news generated far less work. In fact, by the afternoon, Ozzie found time to begin sifting through all of the papers that he had amassed in his desk drawers and cupboard during his time at the Council. Rob left him to his tedious task and called on Nora Allen in Democratic Services to see how things were going with the administration of the South Titbury by-election vote, which was taking place that day.

Her two junior colleagues, Sally and Katrin, were busy finalising the processing of postal ballots and then planned to travel across to the community centre in Titbury to count the rest of the vote when the polls closed at 10 PM.

Rob doubted whether the local press would attend the count as it was such a foregone conclusion and involved working late at night. Bearing that in mind, he was tempted to give it a miss himself but he thought it would be best to ask Nora for her opinion. He found that she had already considered the issue and had been intending to phone him to stand him down,

'I don't think that the reporters will bother travelling to Titbury to report on such a formality, Rob, especially as there are heavy rain showers forecast for tonight. You could argue that Roger offering his services for free might sway more people to vote Lib Dem, but the Tories have been hot favourites since the day that Charles Horsfield threw in the towel, and everyone thinks that they're home and hosed. Also there's not another WHIP independent candidate stepping into Horsfield's shoes to upset the apple cart.'

'But there are other independents standing for election, aren't there?'

'Yes, there's two of them. One is a woman fixated on improving the bus services regardless of the cost, and the other is a nutter who goes by the name of Poetry Mc Poet Face. His main goal seems to be that everyone should speak in rhyme for some unknown reason. His campaign leaflet is rather good, actually - *Let your mind be free, and vote for me. I'll work like hell and serve you well.* It has a nice ring to it, don't you think?'

After chuckling about the poetic crank, Nora and Rob agreed that he wouldn't need to attend the vote count. She promised to call him at about 11.30 PM to provide the result, enabling him to post the details on the Council website in quick time.

Chapter XXXIV

Snow snow Ric Ric snow ...

Rob was contacted by Nora at the time they had agreed and, as expected, she confirmed that the Conservative candidate, Wayne Kerr, had won the South Titbury by-election by a very comfortable margin. He also learned from Nora that *The Shark* and his gang had been rather put out when they turned up to celebrate with the victor and discovered that there were no media reps to record the event for posterity. Apparently, Ric was threatening to have Rob's guts for garters in the morning.

Nora mentioned that Jim Harvey had attended the count to show support for the Lib Dem candidate Will Rafferty even though they both knew that he hadn't stood a chance. Her highlight of the night had been the poetic contender signing off with a flourish when he declared that *The Tories have just pulled a flanker - they've won it with a guy called Wayne Kerr.* Apparently, his jolly jape hadn't gone down too well with the Conservative element at the venue.

Before he went to bed, Rob grabbed his work laptop and published the details of the result on the WDC website. He then put the finishing touches to a media release that he had drafted earlier (assuming a Tory win) and sent it to the usual distribution. Rob noticed that Twitter feeds for Cllr Sharkey - and his trusty lieutenant, Cllr Lesley Ashurst - were already showing signs of life, with photos of Wayne spraying a bottle of champagne around the hall against a backcloth of party poppers going off.

As he was drifting off to sleep, he reflected that the Tories were now just one victory away from taking over the Council. Another gain in the East Woldchester by-election, due in three weeks, would sound the death knell for the Lib Dem/Labour Coalition and usher in a more radical populist regime.

Rob wondered yet again whether he would still be in a job if Cllr Sharkey took over as Leader of WDC. Normally, the prospect of being sacked would have concerned him immensely but the mere thought of *The Shark* calling the shots suggested that it might be a welcome relief to pack his bags and find a new job. His relationship with Sandy was steering him on an upward curve and he was hopeful that it might withstand him moving to another part of the country. He trusted that both of their mothers wouldn't make life too difficult for them if things turned more serious, so anything was possible.

Rob had forgotten to switch off his mobile phone because of the flurry of activity prior to his usual bedtime, and it sparked into life just as he was almost dead to the world. He was inclined to ignore it when he realised that the display listed the caller as Sandy. Rubbing his bleary eyes, he pressed receive to hear her dulcet Scottish tones,

'Hi Robster, I realise that it's a wee bit late but I've just had a great idea and I wanted to share it with you straight away. I thought you might still be awake because I just saw the by-election result and assumed that you might be tidying up the admin.'

'Hi Sand. Yes, I was just releasing the announcement on the website. Fire away.'

'Well, we've got a school skiing trip coming up in Austria in two months' time and there's a spare place for another adult supervisor if you fancy it. You don't have to commit right now but I do need to know by close of play tomorrow.'

'Of course I'll come. Just tell me when it is and I'll be there. I've got loads of leave due and I normally tend to short change myself and just lose it. Mind you, I hope I won't be renewing the acquaintance of any of those teenage horrors that had a go at me when I did that careers talk at the school.'

'Em, er yes, a few of them might be going, but we'll still get to spend lots of time together and I can handle those monsters if they step out of line.'

Rob was sufficiently placated and he was about to close down the call and drift off to his slumbers when Sandy added .

'Oh,, I expect you'll have heard about Ozzie's Dad standing as the Labour candidate in the East Woldchester by-election?'

All at once, Rob wasn't feeling so tired and he roused himself from his slouch,

'Well I never! He must have scraped in with his nomination just before the deadline yesterday. Ozzie hasn't said a word to me about this. He told me once that his Dad lived in that part of town but I don't really know much else about him.'

'Oh, my Mum knows Bertie quite well. That's why we heard all about it. He used to be her partner when she did Scottish country dancing at the local church hall. Bertie's a widower and I think he's quite sweet on Mum. In fact, he's asked her to help with the leafleting.'

'Good heavens. What else do you know about him?'

'What I gather from Mum is that he's in his mid-sixties and retired - but he's still very active and seems to have lots of things on the go, especially painting and decorating jobs for beer money. She says he's well liked in the neighbourhood and he won an award from The Examiner a couple of years ago for creating a community garden. He's been a Labour Party member for ever and a day and tried to get Mum to attend one of their meetings - but she told him that life was too short for that sort of nonsense! From what she's told me, I can't imagine him having many skeletons in the closet so there's probably not a lot of dirt that his rivals can dig up.'

'Let's hope not - it's shameful what the Tories did to Fred Clark. The poor man didn't deserve such shoddy treatment after his heroics. I bet he wishes that he'd turned down the chance to represent the Lib Dems and settled for a quiet life in his new home instead.'

'Is his campaign really dead in the water now?'

'Not completely. But it will take a lot of hard work to convince enough voters that he's not a sex-craved philanderer after all the accusations that Sharkey and co have flung at him.'

'You never know. He's really handsome when he smartens himself up, and the family who thanked him for saving their daughter's life have been on the local radio saying that they're standing behind him despite the bad mouthing.'

They talked a while longer about other issues of mutual interest, and Rob realised that they were behaving like a serious long-term couple. He was delighted that Sandy had wanted to speak to him before retiring for the night and, when the call ended, he experienced a soothingly warm tingle inside which lulled him to sleep.

During the night, however, Rob's slumbers were not so serene. He had a vivid dream which involved Cllr Sharkey and an unruly mob of students from the local comprehensive hurtling down a steep hill on skis while towing him and Sandy on a sled. The hapless couple had no control over the contraption whatsoever and were becoming increasingly alarmed as the descent steepened and the number of their persecutors dwindled until *The Shark* was the only one remaining. The tormentor in chief quickened the pace before releasing his guide rope and left them to their own devices on the runaway toboggan.

The petrified pair were hurtling downhill with no means of controlling their descent, and screamed loudly as they narrowly avoided a stand of conifers poking through the snow. Just as it looked like they were heading for a dark abyss at terrifying speed, the intrepid Fred Clark suddenly appeared, whooshing across their path on a monoski, and he expertly steered them towards a safe haven in their hour of need.

When they had reached safer terrain, the late Cllr Wharton mysteriously appeared bearing mugs of Gluhwein for Rob, Sandy and their gallant rescuer. The party then sat around in the winter sunshine discussing the perfidious antics of Cllr Sharkey while the snow glistened all around them and everything was calm and bright. All of a sudden, their peace was disturbed by an ominous rumbling noise, and Fred looked instinctively towards the top of the mountain. Once he'd assessed the situation, he sounded a warning that Sharkey had regained his starting point and had triggered an avalanche that was gathering pace quickly. They all tried to run as fast as they could manage to outpace the advancing wall of thick snow and ice but they were fighting a losing battle and ..

Rob woke up with a start and it took him a while to realise that he was tucked up in bed safe and sound. Ric Sharkey had never intruded into his slumbers previously and his gruesome intervention in Rob's night time routine impressed upon him that he would be best advised to move to another place of work should the upcoming by-election result in another Tory gain.

Chapter XXXV

Under starter's orders...

The three weeks leading up to the East Woldchester by-election were marked by frenzied activity on behalf of the main contenders. The Lib Dems were trying desperately to restore the reputation of Fred Clark and hoped that an initial burst of indignation about his extra-marital affairs would be tempered by his engaging manner when people met him face to face. As predicted, his shallow appreciation of political issues wasn't a major handicap on the stump provided he was accompanied by a knowledgeable minder, and many women voters took a shine to him once they got chatting on their doorsteps.

The Conservatives were running a very effective campaign to support their candidate, a local florist called Christine Suggett who bore a striking resemblance to a well known actress who was regarded as a *national treasure*. On close inspection, Ms Suggett wasn't by any means the usual Tory patrician that voters might have expected; she could best be described as a practical type, with a supportive husband, two nice kids, and an admirable sense of duty and purpose. Nadine Hurley had been instrumental in finding the right sort of person for the ward and was convinced that Christine would appeal to the average voter in Woldchester.

Labour Party activists were equally confident that Bertie Burton would be the victor, and trusted that the late Cllr Wharton's legacy of goodwill might carry the day for him. Bertie was tipped to curry favour with the older generation, and his socialist backers took heart from the fact that the grey brigade was usually more inclined to turn up and vote on the day. Bertie himself was not fazed by the attention he was receiving, and he took great delight in posing for photographs with his paintbrush and roller to emphasise his dedication to hard graft.

As each day went by, the importance of the occasion intensified for the Tories in particular. They were desperate to wrest control of the seat in the knowledge that defeat at the hands of either the Lib Dems or the Socialists would ensure the existing Coalition hung on to its majority by a whisker. Nadine instructed the Conservative party activists to leaflet every house in the ward every other day, and the creatives in her team were working all hours to come up with fresh reasons for spurning alternative candidates.

Rubbishing the Coalition record in power was easy for the Tories, but they felt that they needed a new line of attack to dispel any remaining threat from Fred Clark. Eventually, Nadine resorted to rooting out another one of his former conquests who dated him when he was driving trucks up north. He didn't appear to have fathered any children with her, but news of yet another affair reinforced the notion that he was a despicable cad.

However, the biggest threat to a Conservative gain was posed by the Labour candidate Bertie Burton, and both Nadine and Ric were stumped when they were ferreting around for ways to damage his chances. Out of the blue, Ric received an unsolicited call from a notorious local gossip who alleged that Burton had left his last full-time job prematurely following suspicions that he was short changing his employer. He had been working as an office manager at a builder's merchants at the time and there was a mysterious dip in profits that was never fully explained.

Ric wanted to dish the dirt as soon as the information came to light but Nadine was concerned that they might come a cropper if they spread salacious rumours without obtaining more corroboration of what amounted to mere tittle tattle. She advised patience when she met up with Ric and Cllr Lesley Ashurst to discuss the next stage of the campaign strategy. Lesley agreed with Nadine's line immediately and backed her tentative approach to the hilt even though Ric was chomping at the bit to dish the dirt,

`We need to do a hell of a lot more investigating to tighten things up on this one, Ric, and I doubt whether it's really worth Nadine's while putting in all that extra effort at this stage of the game. You can tell that she's really knackered and needs a bit of a rest - so how about letting this one go eh?'

Nadine would normally have promised to go the extra mile on the research front but she really was exhausted and pleaded,

'Ric dear, I've hit a bit of a wall, if I'm being honest, and it sometimes takes an unfeasibly long while to bottom out rumours when finance is involved. You know, dearest, I've got a nose for these things and I have genuine concerns that this whole fraud story might be a fairytale. More to the point, if we jump the gun and make an error we could end up with Bertie suing our backsides off for defamation. We can't just recycle this sort of flimsy tat from an unreliable source.'

Lesley added helpfully,

'Don't forget that old Mr Burton is a really popular bloke. He's also operating on his home patch, so it makes sense for us to back away from going for the jugular when we're on shaky ground.'

Ric wasn't suited at all and was acting like a spoiled child when both women continued to urge a climbdown. Lesley sensed that he was going to explode with rage, and she was intensely disappointed when he finally declared,

'Don't get me wrong. I can see where you're both coming from ... but it's obvious that Bertie's doing rather well in the opinion polls we've collated. If he wins the ward for Labour, we know it's odds on that he'll join forces with the Lib Dems - and then our chance of gaining power will be gone for a long while. That's why my gut reaction is to run with the allegations against Bertie right now provided we finesse them a bit, and forget about checking the facts too much. This one's much too big to lose.'

Lesley was furious when she realised that he was refusing to back down, and she stormed out of the room before she said something she might regret. She only hoped that Nadine would exercise her excellent persuasive skills to put *The Shark* back in his box once he had cooled down.

In the past, bringing Ric to heel would have been a formality for Nadine, but she was beginning to fear that the creature she had unleashed was not as malleable as she had originally anticipated. Instead of battering away at his adamantine resolve to no avail, she left him to stew for a while and resorted to scouring Bertie's social media postings over a number of years. She was on the hunt for any little chink in his armour that might present an alternative obstacle to his progress.

Eventually, after a lot of scrolling through online comments focusing mostly on Bertie's decorating skills and his prowess on the dance floor, Nadine managed to unearth an ancient rant from the man himself on his Facebook account, attacking the privileges enjoyed by the Royal Family. Republican leanings were not a big deal, especially in comparison with juicy allegations about potential fraudulent behaviour, but at least the evidence was watertight.

Armed with Bertie's horse's mouth hostility towards the monarchy, she pleaded with Ric to throw his weight behind exploiting that situation instead. She argued coherently that there would be a sufficient number of royalists in East Woldchester who might take offence when they were informed about Bertie's intense antipathy. Ric was extremely sceptical about her suggested line of attack given the number of scandals that had engulfed the House of Windsor over the years, but he finally gave ground when Nadine stressed that they could brand Bertie as a closet anarchist with a mad desire to burn down Buckingham Palace.

The LIb Dems still hoped that Fred Clark would prevail despite his recent come-uppance in the media, and threw as much support as possible behind his bid to win the seat. In comparison with the bad vibes in South Titbury, there was less public aversion to Jim Harvey's regime in Woldchester. Nevertheless,the tabloids had done a lot of damage when they turned the tables on Fred, and the Tories continued to hammer home his moral turpitude in the flyers that they were dropping through letterboxes. Perhaps the most damaging Tory campaign leaflet depicted the Lib Dem contender as a *despicable love rat* complete with whiskers and a tail, and it carried the bellicose slogan *Keep vermin at bay in East Woldchester.*

By the eve of the vote, many residents were sick of the sight of party activists from across the political spectrum knocking on their doors and feeding them with propaganda. Volunteers were working feverishly until the last minute to boost the turnout and their efforts resulted in a distinctly febrile atmosphere in the area ahead of the big day.

Back at Reilly Road, Nora Allen and her team were busy processing postal votes and she noticed that the volume of returns was much greater than the amount they had dealt with during the previous by-election in South Titbury. She told Rob about the heightened interest and it confirmed to him that many of the ward constituents were aware of the significance of the by-election and the role they would be playing in deciding the future direction of the entire Council. A national tabloid had picked up on this issue, while searching for more material to sustain the Fred Clark sex scandal, and its headline declared: *Can Captain Fred win by the seat of his underpants?*

Chapter XXXVI

And they're off!

At 7 AM on the morning of the by-election, the doors opened at the polling station which had been set up in the Woldchester Assembly Rooms, and members of the public began to exercise their right to vote in person.

From the outset, it was obvious that the turnout was going to be relatively high, and volunteers from the ranks of the Lib Dems, Tories and Labour continued working all hours to encourage voter participation, including the offer of transport to and from the Assembly Rooms on request. Others were on hand to query the choice that electors had made when they were exiting the polling station, enabling them to gauge the way the political wind was blowing - assuming, of course, that respondents were telling the truth!

Jim Harvey was quite serene on the day in the knowledge that the Lib Dems had done their utmost to restore Fred Clark's credibility, while being aware that they couldn't perform miracles. The Labourites, with Cllr Dave Dillon leading the charge, were praying that Bertie Burton would prevail, and hoping that last-minute Tory attempts to brand their man as an anti-Royalist iconoclast would not be a show stopper. To his credit, Bertie didn't react to the Tory jibes and was becoming adept at changing the subject when his republican leanings were questioned.

The most jittery person on the scene was *The Shark*; after all his attempts to nobble the other two front runners, Ric still remained concerned that Christine Suggett might not appeal to enough voters to triumph. His band of close associates were struck by his skittish behaviour as he did his rounds like a bear with a sore head. His mournful face appeared more drawn than usual, betraying a lack of sleep and loss of appetite, and Nadine subtly arranged for a couple of minders to keep him away from voters whenever possible on account of his dark mood.

As the day progressed, the Assembly Rooms became increasingly busy, and the presiding officer estimated that the number of votes cast would be remarkably high. Aside from feverish efforts by all parties to drag people from their hearths to the polling station, the weather had also helped to boost the numbers because predicted rain showers hadn't materialised. Nora Allen popped along during the late afternoon to assess the lie of the land for herself, and decided to supplement her support team to ensure that they could verify the votes and then count them in a speedy fashion once the poll closed at 10 PM.

Finally, the clock in the Assembly Rooms indicated that the poll was closing and Nora and her experienced team began the verification process. They were able to operate in quick time because all the votes had been cast at one venue, and there was no need to transport ballot boxes from outlying locations. As they toiled like demons , a large number of attendees gathered, including candidates and their friends and many serving councillors. Several

WDC officials were also present - including Rob Cummings, Meera Chopra, and Viv Bushby - and the two familiar reporters, Tom and Lena, were prowling around the venue taking photographs and conducting interviews for their live blogs.

As with all elections, verification was the necessary first step to produce an accurate result. This meant that Nora's team had to count the papers in each ballot box to make sure that the totals matched the official numbers that had been issued, as stated on the ballot paper account. If the numbers didn't tally, they would have to identify and explain the source of the variance or, alternatively, recount the contents of any rogue box at least twice. Fortunately, there were no glitches and Nora was very pleased to announce that the verification process was complete and that her team would soon begin counting the votes given to each candidate.

At this stage in the proceedings, the onlookers moved closer to the tables where the counting was going to take place because they wanted to gain a rough idea of the number of votes being apportioned to each party. There was a murmur of excited conversation when the process got underway and a clear pattern began to emerge within a matter of minutes. As expected, the Independent hopeful campaigning for improvements to cat protection, Lord Mew Mew, wasn't really in the running, but the piles of votes cast for Fred Clark were also disappointingly small. On the other hand, the ballot papers favouring the Tory and Labour Party candidates were piling up and it was soon evident that there was going to be a very close outcome.

Nora was aware of the attention being focused on her charges as the counting progressed, and made sure that they were not distracted from the job in hand by reminding everyone to respect the *cordon sanitaire* established between their tables and the public. As the tally for each box was recorded, she ensured that all the subtotals were recorded meticulously in readiness for them to be added together to produce the final result.

When the moment finally came to tot up the numbers, Nora reckoned that the result wasn't conclusive enough to call at that juncture. Her calculations showed that the Tories had amassed 3,712 votes, the Labour total was 3,707, the Lib Dems were on 603, and Lord Mew Mew had a surprising 43 backers (she quietly amused herself by referring to them as 'stray votes'). Those gathering for the announcement of the result were informed that the numbers were too tight at the top to deliver a final verdict, and it came as no surprise when Nora advised them that a recount was necessary.

The Democratic Services ladies had been half expecting an extra shift halfway through the original count, and got back to work again after a well deserved coffee break, taking special care to allocate each paper correctly. Within an hour it was time for Nora to do another summing up and, this time around, the numbers showed that Lord Mew Mew had retained his 43 votes and the Lib Dems had attracted four more to bring their total to 607. This anomaly benefited the Tories who only declined by one to 3,711 whereas the Labour vote dropped to 3,704. After Nora called the contenders to her desk, Bertie Burton conceded that he had lost the battle to Christine Suggett, and it was agreed that Nora would make the result known officially.

When she did so, the Tory supporters in the hall roared their appreciation and there were hugs all around in their camp. Bertie Burton was a model of decorum in defeat and congratulated the victor courteously before leaving the venue with his supporters trailing behind him. Fred Clark was also a humble loser and wished Christine Suggett the best of luck; he was thanked by Jim Harvey who assured him that he had done a great job in trying circumstances. Lord Mew Mew disappeared from view and was never seen in the area again.

Cllr Sharkey was ecstatic and kept punching the air like a madman. He was beyond coherence when he was babbling about the *glorious victory* and Nadine forced him into an adjoining room to calm him down with a cup of chamomile tea. She noticed that the news reporters were all over Christine like a rash and was relieved that they weren't too bothered about seeking Ric's immediate reaction to the result. Nadine feared that her partner would have come across as a manic interviewee in such a hyped up state and she resolved to keep him away from the action as long as possible.

He was sweating profusely while he drank his tea so Nadine sat him down and took off his jacket. As she did so, a bottle of pills spilled out of the pocket and, to her dismay, she realised that the idiot had doped himself up to the eyeballs on a cocktail of stimulants. Not for the first time of late, she wondered whether she had really chosen the right proxy to fulfil her political ambitions, and there was a marked frostiness in her tone when she told Ric to rest and take deep breaths as he tried to pull himself around.

When Ric was semi-prone on a chair, Nadine nipped outside through a side door and lit up a sly cigarette to steady her nerves. As she was smoking outside while leaning on a window ledge, she kept telling herself that Ric was on the cusp of great things and that she had the strength of purpose to stop him crashing and burning.

At first she didn't see Meera Chopra, but a slight movement in the shadows caught her attention and the two women were unexpectedly facing each other in the gloom. Meera had decided to take the night air to escape the heavy atmosphere in the hall, and she couldn't resist broaching the result with Nadine when she saw that the Tory svengali was sitting alone with a rather disconsolate expression on her face,

'I suppose congratulations are in order, Ms Hurley. But, unless I'm mistaken, you don't really look like you're too excited about the result.'

Nadine stubbed out her fag in an instant, and switched on her happy face,

'I'm over the moon, actually. It's just a bit hard to take it all in at the moment. Ric's the same - he's taking a break because he needs to de-stress a bit.'

'I expect you're both worn out after all your skullduggery during the campaign. A lot of people know about the lengths you went to when you were hunting for votes. Poor Mr Burton never harmed a fly and I'm sure Mr Clark didn't deserve such a mauling in the gutter press. You've caused a lot of upset to achieve your aims and I hope it's been worth it.'

'That's a load of nonsense. If there are character flaws to be exploited then it's perfectly okay for us to highlight them. Simple as that.'

'Well, it's a good job that you didn't look closer to home when you were trying to find faults - I have strong suspicions that your partner is a bit of a racist on the quiet, and he can be very antagonistic towards the WDC officers to the point that he won't listen to reason. I don't know what your personal game plan is but I wouldn't bet on *The Shark* doing everything that you expect. The word is that you have friends in high places, and I wouldn't be surprised if they start to warn you off this guy when he settles in as the Leader at Reilly Road.'

That was Meeera's parting shot and she strode off before Nadiine could summon up an acerbic riposte. The Tory Svengali hadn't expected Meera to adopt such a subversive attitude towards the incoming leadership at WDC, and the legal advisor's candid comments had rattled her more than she expected, probably because they echoed her own fears about RIc.

Meera would normally have kept her own counsel but she was emboldened because she had already put out the feelers for other jobs and was very confident that she would find suitable work elsewhere. When she returned to the main body of the hall to help the Democratic Services team pack away, the Tory supporters were still very much in evidence basking in their success.

Nadine followed hard on Meera's heels and informed the revellers that she had arranged for late night Prosecco and snacks to be served down the road at the Tory party HQ. As she expected, they hastened from the building to continue their celebrations, but Nadine surprisingly excused herself and Ric and said that they had urgent follow-up business to discuss. Turning swiftly on her heels, she returned to the darkened room that was the resting place of the new Leader of the Council and told him that it was time for bed - but not in the sexy sense. He looked crestfallen when he realised that he was missing out on a victory celebration bash, but she could tell that he was dead on his feet and he willingly followed her to the car like a little lost lamb in need of some TLC. .

Chapter XXXVII

Steward's inquiry

The day after the count, a rejuvenated RIc breezed into the Comms Office at Reilly Road like a dog with two tails. *The Shark* was now on a high following Chistine Suggett's success and addressed the two occupants of the room cheerily,

'Good morning, gentlemen. I imagine that you're catching up on all the news coverage of our magnificent victory last night. I'll be back later with a celebratory video that you can issue on the website, Rob. From now on, I'll be overseeing your tasks directly so I expect we'll be working together a lot more closely - well, at least until I review my comms requirements and decide whether you're the right fit for the job. Anyway, ta ta for now.'

Rob dreaded the prospect of Ric breathing down his neck at all hours of the day, and envied Ozzie who was packing away his possessions into a cardboard box prior to leaving the Council for pastures new. Ozzie was attempting to weed out all the rubbish that had accumulated in his desk over time and he fished out the *Dyno Active* literature that Joe Baxter had supplied. He flung the offensive material across to Rob's desk and said,

'I think you might have to pay more attention to this charlatan now that the new Tory regime is nigh. *The Shark* will have carte blanche to introduce Baxter's vile monitoring system, and it's odds on that he'll want you to sing its praises in public.'

Rob reluctantly picked up the brochure like it was a mouldering dog turd, and leafed through it at random, trying not to dwell on the true horror of the shape of things to come. He had just reached the blurb towards the end when he sat up and yelled,

'Oh. My. God! Bingo By Jingo! - at long last! Eureka! I've just realised where I first saw Nadine Hurley - look Oz, her photo is staring me in the face on the page displaying mugshots of company directors.'

Even though he wasn't always the tastiest sandwich in the picnic, Ozzie twigged the implication straight away,

'That's not a good look for Cllr Sharkey is it? He's been plugging an enterprise that benefits the financial interests of his partner, if this brochure is to be believed.'

Rob analysed the situation,

'Well I guess Ric doesn't necessarily have to state what Nadine gets up to on his WDC official register of interests statement, but it looks a bit smelly if he's going around trying to drum up trade which would boost her income. He certainly hasn't disclosed this connection to anyone as far as I know, and I'm not sure that this embarrassing coincidence would go down too well with any of the WDC councillors if it came to light.'

As Ozzie and Rob were unravelling the mysteries of the power brokers behind the *Dyno Active* project, the Environment and Communities Head of Service Albert Suddick was at his desk reorganising waste collection schedules to accommodate planned new housing estates in Woldchester and Titbury. His careful calculations were interrupted by a knock on the door and RIc trotted into his office with a cheesy grin plastered over his weasel-like face.

The Shark may have been beside himself with joy following the decisive vote in East Woldchester but he was by no means content to rest on his laurels. Albert could tell that the Leader in waiting was on the scent of yet another bad news story to hammer the outgoing regime. Anticipating a rich new source of doom and despondency, courtesy of the waste management department, Ric said,

'I got your call to come and see you as soon as possible, Al. I expect the national fly tipping figures are out eh?'

Albert looked up from his calculations and replied coolly,

'Yes, Cllr Sharkey, they've just been released officially. Unfortunately, they're almost as bad as we feared, and our Council has gone further down the league table.'

'Dear oh dear - that really is a shame. Well, come on, Al, spill the beans - how bad is bad, eh? '

'Before I do that, I must explain that my name is Albert and that I asked you to visit my office for another reason primarily.'

'Eh? What's that then, Al? Have we gone down in the recycling charts too?'

'No. It's more about your insistence on the zero tolerance treatment we should apply to fly tippers.'

249

'Yes, that's right. You know full well that I'm always fully behind that measure. Now that a competent team is taking over at the top table, I'm confident that we can do a better job of nailing these louts. Look Al , er Albert, we have to prosecute offenders every time to set a strong example. Surely you're not disagreeing with that are you?'

'No Cllr Sharkey, I couldn't agree with you more. It's just that we found a load of builder's rubble dumped by the side of the road near Little Chipping the other day and our guys did some sleuthing. They turned up these papers while they were sifting through the crud.'

Albert passed a polythene bag to Ric containing envelopes addressed to Mr R Sharkey, various receipts traceable to his credit card and some of his handwritten notes. There was absolutely no doubt that the items had originated from *The Shark's* study. Ric was completely baffled and, after a few moments of ominous silence, he finally asked,

'Is this some kind of stupid prank, Albert? How the hell did this stuff end up in a fly tip?'

'You tell me, Cllr Sharkey. It looks like someone in your household hired a firm to remove waste from your premises and didn't check whether they were a registered waste carrier licensed by the Environment Agency. It often happens, and residents are completely floored when they realise that a company they trusted has only driven as far as the nearest convenient hedgerow and slung the entire load in there.'

'Ah, well that explains everything. Nadine was mad keen for me to add a conservatory to my home and we've just finished with the builders. She told me the other day that she'd found a little man with a van on the Internet and he came and cleared away the mess left behind. I expect that she threw away some of our more personalised waste at the same time. No harm done then as far as we're concerned eh? Maybe I can get Nadine to trace who she hired to do the deed so we can prosecute the little shit - she's awfully good at digging out info.'

'Well, that's very reassuring to know, but I'm afraid that householders are just as liable as the carriers when it comes to fly tipping. According to the law, residents are responsible for making sure their waste is disposed of safely and legally. Under the terms of the Environmental Protection Act, you could face a charge of up to £5,000 if it appears that you failed to take reasonable measures to ensure that the company you engaged is authorised to do the job. In other words, ignorance on the part of the resident is no excuse.'

Ric was flustered and, for a rare moment, he didn't really know what to say. Finally, he croaked out,

'So what you're saying is that Nadine could be fined a small fortune for colluding in illegal dumping? Why, that's fucking ridiculous.'

'Well maybe your partner is at fault but, strictly speaking, the name we have in relation to the offence is yours. So if we pursue this matter in line with our zero tolerance approach then I'm afraid that you're in the dock, Cllr Sharkey.'

Ric couldn't believe what was happening. He began clutching at straws,

'Hang on a moment, you know fine well that I'm innocent - and poor Nadine has been stitched up as well. Surely, there's a means of knocking this farce on the head? I'm on the verge of being anointed as Leader of the whole shebang here, for Christ's sake.'

'Cllr Sharkey, all I can say is that the incident report will be forwarded to our Head of Legal Affairs, Meera Chopra and, in light of any appeal from yourself, she will be the final arbiter in deciding whether to pass this matter to the courts.'

'Bloody hell. She's the last person I would want to decide my fate. I had a go at her the other day about her tardiness in responding to Freedom of Information requests and she wasn't best pleased.'

'Well, I can assure you that she's always completely impartial when it comes to making legal decisions. But, you know what they say? What goes around comes around. So I suggest that you cosy up to Meera and try to convince her that this offence shouldn't be referred to the police. Good luck with that.'

Ric was finding it difficult to take in what had just happened. He had been on cloud nine a few moments ago and now, in the blink of an eye, he was digging dirt among the dead men.

While Ric's omnishambles was unfolding, Nadine Hurley had been busy buying luxury food items at the deli counter in her local supermarket. She was organising a small function to celebrate her partner's forthcoming coronation as the head honcho at WDC and her next stop was the hair studio. She'd invited a select group of friends and influencers to Ric's home that evening, and had chosen a smorgasbord of culinary delights plus a crate of Bollinger to mark the momentous occasion. She had just paid for the goods when her mobile phone rang. Seeing that the caller was Ric, Nadine refrained from letting the phone's voicemail kick in and answered swiftly,

'Ric darling, my man of the hour! How does it feel to be the future king of Woldwater District Council?'

'Whoa, Nadine - not so fast. I've run into a spot of bother and I need your advice to get around it.'

He explained the fly tip dilemma and her major role in dropping him in the brown stuff, expecting her to suggest an ingenious way to solve the problem. Nadine listened attentively and then replied,

'Hmm, that's all very unfortunate, Ric darling. I'll see if I can locate the lowlife who tipped our waste but it won't be easy - he knocked on the door and offered to clear things up when I was in a bit of a rush so I didn't even see the registration number of his van. Now, moving on to more important things... I've sorted all the goodies for our do tonight and I just wanted to make sure that...'

'Nadine. I don't think you've got your head around the gravity of the situation here! Unless I can dodge this waste dumping bullet we won't be having any sort of fuckin' party at all. I might even have to step down from the Council if the worst comes to the worst. I really need your excellent investigative skills to see if you can nail anything tasty on Meera Chopra. That might persuade her to go easy on me.'

Nadine paused again to gather her wits and then answered calmly,

'Look Ric. Enough is enough. I'm done with all that jiggery-pokery for a while and I certainly don't want to go sniffing around a person like Meera - the word is that she can be a bit of a viper on the quiet. She had a quiet little chat with me last night and it was obvious that she wasn't at all impressed by the way we conducted our electioneering. I'm sorry, love, but you're on your own on this one.'

As soon as she hung up, she concluded that all her hard work grooming RIc for success had been in vain. His increasingly erratic behaviour had become a cause for concern and a voice in her head had been urging her to ditch her protege for quite a while.Being of a practical mind, she shrugged her shoulders and called the delectable Wayne Kerr to see if he was free for a picnic lunch. After all, she didn't want all of her foodie treats going to waste.

Chapter XXXVIII

The King is dead, long live the Queen ..

Ric had the distinct feeling that he was a naughty schoolboy who had been ushered into the headmaster's study. He was asked to sit on a hard plastic chair in Meera's office while she considered how to proceed, given his involvement in a *slam dunk* fly tipping offence. To her credit, Meera was able to rise above her contempt for the man and was a model of rectitude as she ploughed her way through Albert Suddick's report on the incident. Finally, she raised her eyes to make contact with the miscreant and declared,

'Well, it's clear that we'll have to issue a fixed penalty notice to Ms Hurley in the first instance. She's already admitted that she hired a rogue waste removal firm so she'll have to bear some of the responsibility for the offence and pay a fine. As for you, Cllr Sharkey, well you're guilty by association so one could argue that you should also be subject to some form of reprimand. My understanding is that the Leader of the Council has to be beyond reproach and I honestly think that you should now consider whether you fit that profile on the back of this misdemeanour.'

Ric was irked by her suggestion and decided to go on the offensive by retorting abrasively,

'And what if I tell you to shove that suggestion up your Asian backside, Ms Chopra?'

'Hang on, there's no need to get personal here. I just think that it might be appropriate for you to convene a meeting of the councillors in your party and assess the way ahead for your administration once I've furnished them with details of the fly tip incident.'

'But this is all down to Nadine, for God's sake. Surely you can't blame me for something that she did when I had no idea what was going on? You know, I reckon old Horsfield wasn't far wrong about you - your lot have absolutely no right to come over here and dictate how we should live our lives in this country. You should be our servants and not our bloody masters. Now if that's us done, you'll have to excuse me because I have a Council to run if you haven't noticed.'

Meera ignored the racial bigotry and pressed on,

'Before you go, there is one more thing we need to touch on, Cllr Sharkey. I believe that you are a big fan of Joe Baxter's *Dyno Interactive* efficiency programme?'

'Why yes. One of the benefits of gaining a working majority is that we can press on with this brilliant initiative. It beats the living daylights out of that piss poor *Future Journey* nonsense, and will actually make some efficiency savings that will stick. '

'And presumably Nadine would do very nicely as well were you to award the contract to Joe?'

'What the hell do you mean by that? She's had no involvement in our discussions so I think you're barking up the wrong tree.'

Meera enlightened him by handing over the copy of Joe Baxter's promotional literature that Rob had passed to her earlier in the day,

'If you look at the photo montage of the firm's directors on page 11 you will see that your partner has a considerable interest in the success of Mr Baxter's venture. I assume that it slipped her mind when she recommended him to you in the first instance?'

'Oh Christmas with bells on it! Wha.. look, I can assure you that this is all news to me. But again you can't blame me for this one either can you?'

'No not directly. But if this happened to one of your colleagues in the Lib Dems, I'm sure you would acknowledge that the optics are very bad and press for punitive action. All I can say is that it's my duty to pass this information to the Council's Audit and Standards Committee and they will deal with the issue as they see fit.'

Meera's second revelation appeared to take the wind out of Ric's sails and he was markedly less belligerent when he returned to the Leader's suite to consider his options. He tried contacting Nadine on his mobile phone several times and when his calls kept going to voicemail it occurred to him that she really wasn't going to save his skin.

While he was deep in thought about the potential consequences of Nadine's actions, there was a loud tap on the office window and Lesley Ashurst poked her head around the door.

'RIc, we're all waiting. Come on, man, there's tons of work to be done.'

His brain was fully engaged in extricating himself from the mire and he'd forgotten completely about the gathering he had scheduled with his inner circle. He rose from his comfy Eames chair and accompanied Lesley into the meeting room where his acolytes were expecting him to set out plans for the new administration.

From the outset, it was obvious that Ric was not in fine fettle, and his associates presumed that he was still feeling below par, having missed the victory booze up in honour of Christine Suggett. When they delved a little deeper, *The Shark* felt compelled to tell them that he had no health issues, but was extremely concerned about forthcoming revelations regarding Nadine's conduct.

Once he had explained the potential ramifications, he was expecting a welter of sympathy but - to his dismay - it was in short supply once his team had gleaned the basic facts. Previously loyal colleagues castigated him for being such a dupe and insisted that he should step down from the leadership role immediately. One of the most vociferous even suggested that Ric should resign from the Council, but everyone else in the room agreed that it would be a backward step as they would probably lose the resulting by-election and hence their chance to maintain their hard won control of the entire administration.

The arrangement they finally agreed was that Ric would have no direct involvement in the running of the senior leadership within the Tory regime, and would be confined to serving his ward to the best of his abilities. They also insisted that he must stand down when the next full round of Council elections was due.

Lesley Ashurst remained tight-lipped throughout the proceedings; she sensed that karma was catching up with them all as they reaped the whirlwind of their underhand electioneering tactics. She regretted that she wasn't squeaky clean on that score, but Ric's most recent chicanery had made her feel sick to the gills and had led her to question whether she really wanted to be part of the whole set up anymore. Nobody was therefore more surprised than Lesley when the collective pleaded with her to become the new Leader of the Council!

It took a while for Lesley to comprehend the magnitude of their request, and she begged time to weigh up the pros and cons carefully. She took herself off for a walk down by the nearby canal and, after considering the ramifications of the offer, she returned to Reilly Road and agreed to take on the new role. However, she attached an important proviso that she would do things differently in comparison with the regime that Ric Sharkey had been contemplating.

Chapter XXXIX

Happy daze?

A few weeks later, Rob and Meera still remained in post at Woldwater and both had stopped looking for alternative employment elsewhere. Surprisingly, life under Lesley Ashurst was proving to be a much more enjoyable experience than they had dared to anticipate, and they were both regaining a genuine sense of job satisfaction at the end of each working day.

Lesley's desire to achieve positive change at WDC began to take shape during her first 24 hours as the Leader when she extended an olive branch to the Lib Dems by appointing Jim Harvey as her Deputy. She also retained Cllr Hilley as the Chair of the Planning Committee and found a place for Cllr Kettleborough within her new *Rainbow* Cabinet. Another immediate priority had been her lengthy pep talk with Cllr Sharkey, ordering him to refrain from meddling in any of the Council's internal affairs, including a cessation in the submission of inane time-consuming information requests to the hard pressed officers. Councillors and officers also welcomed the swift introduction of a new ethics code which she instigated in liaison with Meera; unlike previous iterations, the revised version had the necessary teeth to tackle any instances of bullying, harassment or racial prejudice within the organisation.

The first meeting of the full Council following her appointment as Leader was a brisk business-like affair conducted in a genial fashion. Most attendees were surprised - nay, even delighted - that it was free from the petty points scoring and political grandstanding that had typified previous gatherings when Cllr Sharkey had been the chief instigator. The highlight of the occasion was the presentation of a special merit award to Fred Clark, recognising his bravery and fortitude, and Lesley was complimented later on her heartfelt speech, which praised his achievements. .

Cllr Starkey was reduced to a mere shadow of the fearsome *bete noire* who had formerly got up the noses of all and sundry. He was seldom seen in Reilly Road and explained that he was busy with his financial consultancy day job, which he had neglected during his quest to become top dog at the Council. As anticipated, Nadine had parted company with the miserable wretch as soon as he'd been emasculated by Lesley and her Cabinet.

Ric's former *inamorata* was now spending a lot of her time with the newly minted Tory councillor Wayne Kerr. Nadine trusted that her latest protege would be more manageable than Ric as he climbed his way up the greasy pole of local politics. She had contacted Lesley to congratulate her on her new role and offered to assist her if required, but so far she hadn't heard back.

Rob was relieved that he would probably be staying at Reilly Road for the foreseeable future, especially as his romance with Sandy was continuing to progress on a very positive upward trajectory. She had dropped a few hints and tips about his appearance and - to the amazement of his colleagues - he was slowly emerging from his beige straitjacket, and the odd bold colour was creeping into his everyday wardrobe. More generally, he exuded a sense of wellbeing and confidence.

Looking back over the ups and downs of the previous few months, he was generally well satisfied with the way things had panned out. In fact, he was so chilled that he was actually looking forward to his week in the Alps with Sandy and fifteen feisty teenagers. Before all that madness got underway, the lovestruck couple were due to undertake a ride in a hot air balloon, courtesy of a heavily discounted offer from Ozzie and Gibbo, who were managing to make a success of their new *Wold-wide Wonder* enterprise.

Apparently, Sandy had always fancied a trip into the stratosphere in a basket supported by a flimsy inflatable. Rob, on the other hand, was terrified at the prospect but he was poised to present her with an engagement ring when they were aloft and he told himself that the ordeal would probably be worth it in the long run. Mrs Staveley had already dropped a hint to him that Sandy regarded him as a *keeper* so he was fairly confident about his proposal being accepted.

He was gazing out of his window at Reilly Road while seeking inspiration for a WDC business newsletter he was compiling about various esoteric government benefits on offer to local firms. At that moment, he realised that he was truly content for the first time in his life and he enjoyed the experience in the knowledge that unforeseen drawbacks would inevitably drag him back to reality at some point.

For the time being, he was happy to plough his little furrow and maintain a serene disposition as he dealt with the media's usual round of queries about dog turds on pavements, missed bin collections, and planning appeals from cantankerous residents. He was just about to call it a day and was looking forward to a social evening at the bowling alley with Sandy, when Lesley rushed into his room and exclaimed,

'Rob, we've got a big problem. That numpty Councillor who I appointed as Head of the Licensing Committee has just been done for a drunk driving offence. We need to sort out our response before the papers get hold of the story...'

Rob smiled wearily and told himself that things might have changed for the better at Reilly Road but there would always be the odd banana skin or two waiting around the corner to keep him and his colleagues on their toes, and maybe even drive them absolutely *loco* on occasions.